Shangri-LOVE

Living The Love Story Within You

ZEMIRAH JAZWIERSKA

Published by
Luminescent Press

Editing by KN Literary Arts and Joni Wilson

Book design by Deborah Perdue,
Illumination Graphics

Library of Congress Control Number: 2016914866
Softcover ISBN: #978-0-9980892-8-7

Dedication

Dedicated to Maiya and Maddie,
who have shown me the nature of unconditional love

Gratitudes

I smile with joy to consider the infinite love that supported me on the journey into sharing Shangri-Love. While this book is a personal sharing of a heartfelt trajectory of wing expansion, I am filled with overwhelming gratitude to each and every soul who has graced my life.

I especially want to thank my parents, Judy and Ed, for providing the love and encouragement to expand my wings. Every single one of my childhood moments was a gift, every one! Each and every single second brought me to where I am in the here and now and in every moment to come. Thank you for introducing me to God and for the inspiration in your steps that lit my way into deeper exploration. Without you, there would be no journey.

To my beloved partner, Todd, for his word artistry, for the inspiration of the name Shangri-Love, and for holding my heart, standing in the fire, and always having an unwavering belief in my wings. You, my dear love, have weathered this hero's journey and you inspire me.

To Jen Walsh, who, for the past twenty-five years has been my kindred spirit, loving me without conditions and always expressing exactly what I am to her, a true friend. To Maiya and Maddie, for showing me what it is to meet life head-on with courage, depth of spirit, and a dedication to greatness of heart. I love you dear ones, with all my soul. To Paul, for teaching me so much about the journey of the heart and what it means to begin and begin again. To all my family, who knew about my wings, long before I even felt them. To Seran, who tenaciously held the mirror up for me to see, again and again and again, that my heart is the brightest part and for introducing me to the myriad ways that I might break through the mental chatter to experience my heart rather than just "know" about it. To Jill, for encouraging me when I meandered into the dark. To Margot and Rita, for weathering the ups and downs of Neverland and beyond.

I am grateful to everyone: the ministers, the practitioners, my prayer partners, the beholders of light, the classmates, the members, and all the other inspirational beings of Mile Hi Church in Lakewood, Colorado. You opened a door within my heart, awakened my soul, enlivened my spirit, and so beautifully held me in consciousness throughout this journey. To John of God, Heather, and Laura, for the healing ministry and dedication to millions; for providing the gateway and journey of deepening into the transformative embodiment of unconditional love. To Carole, for being a wonderful friend and listening to numerous paragraphs in the book proposal phase. To my students, who endeavor to teach me mindful presence each day. To Norie and Toti, my accountability sisters, open to learning and expanding through all the creative endeavors. To my team of literary geniuses: KN Literary Arts (especially Anne who cared for the words on the page and nurtured them into flowing expression), Deborah at Illumination Graphics, Amy at New Shelves, Shannon at Illustrating You, Viki at Expert Insight Publishing, and Christine Kloser, for her generous heart and for lighting up my author soul.

And to all the Prince Charmings in Neverland who braved to date me when I was the Chameleon Princess. I am truly grateful for each one of you and so indebted, for it was in those adventures that I was catalyzed to dive deeper into my soul.

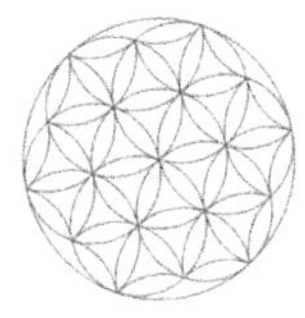

CONTENTS

INTRODUCTION

My heart is awakening. Your heart is awakening. And I believe the heart of all humanity is awakening as well, to our untapped capacity for peace, love, and joy. While each of us is at a different stage of awakening, I feel that we are being called collectively. There's an invitation on the line. And should we RSVP, the possibility exists for greater expression from the heart, a greater depth of living. We are standing, poised at the edge of an expansive experience of grace. All it takes is saying yes to the soul's call to be seen, heard, and honored to expand into a new way of finding love and experiencing love at a deeper level. When we find love, we are no longer hiding behind an image of who and what we think we are supposed to be.

When we *aren't* answering the deep call to love, we are seeking love and joy outside ourselves in a world that is constantly moving the love carrot. The love carrot comes in many forms—it may be work, success, lovers, shopping, food, or any number of things.

Although we each have our own unique love carrot, we are all drawn to love, to the deeper feeling of peace and well-being within us that love is. In our hearts, we are all seeking to love and to experience being loved. Regardless of the stage of our individual awakening to this love, it is the inner impulse inherent in each of us. I believe it's our greatest realization when we get in touch in a deep way, with that part of ourselves that is this essence of love.

This book is my own personal journey of saying YES to my soul's invitation to becoming more joyful and at peace. Once I signed my yes on the dotted line, everything in my life began to shift in the direction of joy. Now, it wasn't like a fairy godmother's bibbidi-bobbidi-boo and I was transformed, riding off to find my prince in a pumpkin-turned-carriage. No. It was a process, a hero's journey of sorts. What started as my search for an external "Shangri-La" culminated in a deepening of my spirit, an awakening of my heart, and an encounter with unparalleled love within myself. This is an ongoing process that continues to this day. None of this awakening was based on an external circumstance (and especially not on a Prince Charming, which you will see I was masterful at seeking). And while certain circumstances may have been much needed catalysts, prompting certain actions on my part, the entire awakening itself was internal.

My search for Shangri-La, a sustainable paradise where I could feel nurtured, loved, safe, and cared for, was not a new one, nor is it unique to me or to one particular culture or gender. The concept of paradise-like societies, or places where compassionate rulers rule and existence is peaceful, beautiful, loving, and prosperous, has been around for an extremely long time. James Hilton made the modern concept of Shangri-La famous in his 1933 novel, Lost Horizon. Over time, Shangri-La became synonymous with an earthly paradise where the "wisdom of humanity" was preserved, ready to usher the world into the golden age. It's thought that Hilton's Shangri-La was based on Tibet's Shambhala, a mythical kingdom located in a valley high in the Himalayas. This just shows that throughout history, humanity has sought a model for an "enlightened society." Legendary kingdoms like Atlantis, Avalon, and Camelot all serve as models, animating the imagination and getting the enlightened juices flowing within us.

I'm here to suggest that the kingdom, the paradise, the mystical place that we have been searching for, can be found! Shangri-La exists! And it exists within each of our own gorgeous hearts. It's my hope that this book will guide you there. I like to call it Shangri-Love, because love is the language of the heart, and this is what I am finding as I dive deeper and deeper within myself and within my own heart. It is a completely self-sustaining place within and requires nothing external for its sustenance, maintenance, or attainment. It's that part of us that is the lotus flower blooming in whatever mud life produces. It's the soul stamina that anchors us in joy. Shangri-Love is the awakened radiant heart. It's universal, and each one of us has the power to access it.

Since you have been drawn to this book, chances are you're feeling the call. This is your call to engage your whole heart, to elevate your spirit, and to deeply develop your capacity for joy. It's your call to connect with the joy within yourself and in the ways you relate with life around you. Your journey will take a committed willingness to stay the course of your heart's deeper unfolding. So activate your unwavering dedication to yourself and turn the page. Do whatever it takes for you to journey deep into to your beautiful heart and follow the path through to the end of the book. It is my heartfelt wish that this journey may offer you a depth of internal shine and a gigantic infusion of joyfulness, allowing you to fully live the love story within you.

Zemirah

CHAPTER 1:

DATING IN NEVERLAND

My divorce from my college sweetheart after fourteen years together went about as well as possible. We had simply grown apart. We parted peacefully as friends, working out an agreement to co-parent our two daughters, then ages eight and five. For the first several months, the girls remained in the family home and we traded ourselves in and out of it, using a rental property as our temporary home. Our arrangement worked for a couple of years, but then everything changed when he remarried. Immediately our channels of communication dried up. From my perspective, it was as if he'd suddenly fallen into a black hole; the man I had known no longer existed. I felt angry and afraid. Nothing remained of my original vision for co-parenting our girls.

I wanted to co-parent these girls throughout their childhood and I wanted to do it with their father! I faced a sadness that was so deep and so intense that I wasn't sure how to deal with it. Gradually, the communication deteriorated even more when I moved out of town for a job in a neighboring city. Eventually, he began to work out of state, and the girls only visited with him on extended vacations.

It was during the time while the girls were still regularly visiting their father that I initiated an Internet dating marathon to distract myself from the pain. It was the pain of suddenly raising my girls alone without the father/partner we used to know and the distress of seeing my girls struggle with understanding the entire situation. I joined five online sites and dated nonstop, sometimes scheduling three or four dates with different men per weekend, carefully setting them up when my daughters had plans. Seeking relief from what felt like an unbearable situation, I entered into a series of mini-relationships birthed in Neverland and raised on Fantasy Island.

I busied myself chasing princes, such as the Hungarian Mason, Peter Pan, the Ashram Hopper, the Infamous Lawyer, the Spine Doctor, the Rock Climber, the Farmer, the Meditation Writer, the Trash Collector, the Marilyn Monroe Lover, and the App Builder. With my neediness at an all-time high, I was a magnet for men who were yoga mat–toting, charming, seductive, ashram visiting, elusive, withdrawn, obsessively introspective, chanting, judgmental, image-driven, guitar-playing, adventurous, intense, defensive, massage giving, emotionally unavailable, meditating, controlling, tai chi–studying, fantasy ridden, angry, and fearful. To be clear, this wasn't a promiscuous sort of quest, but rather a way to fill the time while simultaneously satisfying my needs for distraction and attention. With most of the men on this list, we just went on a date or two and some-times only coffee. In retrospect, it all made sense; those were the signals *I* was sending out, so those were the types of peo-ple I was attracting. I didn't know it at the time, but they were mirroring me back to myself.

I had an urgent desire to find a partner and an equally urgent desire to find alternative sources of comfort. So I simultaneously studied as many forms of wellness and spir-ituality as I could find. I hired a coach, attended work-shops, retreats, and classes; I bought into numerous healing modalities and coaching packages and underwent many forms of bodywork.

On one hand, this intense seeking was another form of distraction. I was grasping for any solution to the deep pain of loss and abandonment, anything to alleviate my suffering and push my sadness away. On the other hand, I was slowly reprogramming my mind and heart for greater openness and awareness. I didn't know it at the time, but I was laying the groundwork for change.

TWO FOR ONE

During this period of my life, I was so open to dating that I occasionally found myself in some unconventional situa-tions. For instance, one night when I was at my girlfriend's house, and she was checking her online dating profile, we realized that the same guy was messaging both of us simul-taneously! So, to have a little fun with it, we both answered his invites. We told him that we were spending the evening together, and he invited us *both* out for a wonderful sushi dinner that same night. (All the while, he boasted to his friends that he was so good at online dating, he'd scored two dates in one!) Things went downhill, however, when during dinner my friend and this man did not see eye to eye. I felt as if I became a referee rather than an attendee of the date.

While they went back and forth on various topics ranging from politics to religion, I enjoyed my sushi and discovered that wasabi is best when eaten in moderation. At the end of the evening my friend and I said goodbye to this gentleman and thanked him for a wonderful meal, but he was too busy taking a selfie with a woman on each arm—proving his genius at landing dates—to hear us.

TAKING OUT THE TRASH

Dating in Neverland, while appearing adventurous and exotic to the outside eye, wasn't all it was cracked up to be—it often left me feeling empty and more alone than if I hadn't been dating at all. Once, I showed up at the Red Rocks Amphitheatre for a first date, and my date was supremely difficult to recognize since he appeared twenty odd years older than what his profile picture had shown. After my shock passed and we greeted, he handed me a huge, black, plastic, Glad bag and some latex gloves and informed me excitedly that we would be cleaning up trash from last night's concert. He animatedly shared his enthusiasm for trash collection and hiked me up to the top boulders to show me "special" trash from 1968. I was less than thrilled to be unexpectedly studying trash on a Saturday afternoon. After he barehandedly picked up several beer cans, some used napkins, and a cigarette butt, he offered his hand to me to assist my traverse of a big rock crevice. I excused myself to take a break in the bathroom and cry. I was trying unsuccessfully to repress the sheer disgust I felt with the gross nature of this escapade. How had my dating life morphed into trash collection? Was this just a giant metaphor from the Universe showing me the state of my inner union?

Not long after that I went out to dinner with a man at a very nice restaurant. I say "went out to dinner" because we met at a restaurant at dinnertime. I expected we'd both order something from the menu, the way one usually does. It turned out that he had other plans, however.

We'd had a long internet conversation and he seemed nice enough; he was a very athletic, attractive "Colorado type" soccer coach/personal trainer who had just relocated to Boulder from Oregon. But things started to get strange when we sat down and he ordered only a bottle of water. He said he wasn't very hungry; did I want to order something? Since I *was* hungry and it was dinnertime and he'd invited me there, I agreed. But I sensed something was very off when he began to ask to taste all of the food on my plate. He spoke about his love for Marilyn Monroe almost exclusively during dinner, with the exception of speaking about his one and only marriage of three months to a woman he met while vacationing in Mexico. I could hardly follow the bouncing ball of the words that were cluttering the sparse atmosphere of our dinner table.

If the stories weren't odd enough, he would often pause in the midst of speaking and while eating off of my plate, turn to me with a strange gleam in his eye and say, "I think we need a hug, don't you think we need a hug?" And then keep on talking as I squirmed to the other end of the fancy semi-circular booth. At the end of the meal he announced that he had "mistakenly" left his wallet in the car and asked me to pay. I couldn't get out of there fast enough! On the way home in the car, I got weepy at the sheer bizarre ickyness of the whole dating process.

Meanwhile, he left message after message on my cell phone stating that he sensed I may have left "upset" and did I want to talk about it? Months later I ran into him while working out at my gym; apparently he was one of the gym's star trainers. I hid behind some towels, but to be honest, I don't think he would've even remembered me.

LOST IN NEVERLAND

What was I doing in Neverland? Getting lost, just like Peter Pan does. I call it Neverland because it was the land where no one was a grownup, including me, and where no relationship was going to grow up either. I even dated my own Peter Pan off and on for two years after my divorce and before I started parenting alone. He was delightful! We sat on rocks, frolicked through nature, cross-country skied at midnight, canoed through snowy valleys, and camped out with the moose, marmots, and killdeer. It was magical. We danced and wrote music, and I think the pupils of my eyes were replaced with actual stars where he was concerned. But it was sheer fantasy. There was nothing to "hang your curtains" on, so to speak.

A good Tinkerbell, I would've drunk poison if he'd asked me to (as Tink does for her Peter). In a way, he *was* my poison. I was hopelessly attached to his ever-wavering acceptance. When he "loved me," I was in heaven. When he "loved me not," I was in hell. And that daisy was constantly being plucked. I got wind of multiple women "friends" who he would text in the middle of our dates. He wasn't satisfied with me and would often tell me so, but I couldn't see beyond the pixie dust in my eyes; I followed him around like a little lost puppy, doting on every beautiful note that streamed out of his guitar. I kept hoping, yearning, for a real relationship with him—I thought if I could just capture more of his attention, we would be golden. There was no hope of finding lasting love, though, when I was searching for it in the land of fantasy to begin with.

ARCHETYPES OF THE HEART

Dating in Neverland was a like a centrifuge for my soul. It was as if all the latent wounds and pain bodies within me were getting massively stirred up so that I could see, feel, and identify them for healing. They were energies that had been ruling my life since childhood and without actually feeling them, they were on course to rule me for the rest of my life, if I didn't actually honor and love them into health.

I didn't know it at the time, but my heart was seeking balance and health. Ambika Wauters, in her book *Chakras and Their Archetypes: Uniting Energy Awareness and Spiritual Growth*, identifies the heart chakra with the ability to "imbue our physical life with the radiance of love, joy, unity, and kinship and stimulates our sense of touch and delight in life." The two energetic patterns of the heart chakra are that of the Actress and the Lover, which can be seen as the shadow and the light side of the heart, respectively. Wauters explains that these energies, when imbalanced, lead to the nonintegrated experiences of "a frozen emotional abyss, enmeshment in codependent relationships and neurotic patterns of resisting love," ones much like my experiences dating in Neverland.

Archetypes, or energetic templates or patterns, help us to decipher the world around us. Think how you would immediately understand what I am talking about if I referred to a woman as *wonder woman* to suggest how she seems to be able to get everything done in her life at once. Or if I called someone a *computer geek*, you would know that I was talking about someone who is a wiz at computers but lacks certain social skills and suaveness when relating to others. I have used archetypes many times to help my brain shift into new ways of being. Dating in Neverland was no exception.

Although I wasn't aware yet, I was operating under the shadow side of my imbalanced, nonintegrated heart chakra. The Actress Archetype, as Wauters goes on to explain "is incapable of real intimacy because it resists feeling its fears and negativity to loving and being loved by another." The dominant activity of this archetype is using drama and conflict to distance itself from others. And love is a mental exercise rather than a function of the heart.

The Actress employs many defense mechanisms in her energetic expression, and I was using most of them to keep a deeper, truer love at bay. Actual love was way too risky; I was, in essence, like a wounded animal who was running, running, running to protect my wounds from being touched and, better yet, healed. By getting enmeshed in these codependent relationship patterns, (by codependent, I mean placing all my worth within the success/fail of relationship and the acceptance/rejection of my date), and projecting my pain onto these Prince Charmings, I could stay protected in a sort of self-imposed isolation, and avoid the deeper vulnerability and purifying experience of real love.

THE ROCKS

Then came the date—a Match.com date—that changed my life forever. It's not what you think. He wasn't "the One." Not even close. We didn't trek through the Himalayas, make out on Venice gondolas, or walk along the Seine holding hands. But it was the date that led to a seismic shift. It hit my relationship reset button once and for all and set me on a course to find my own personal Shangri-La.

My date was a gorgeous, South African investment banker working on Wall Street who'd invited me on a business trip to Australia. We were scheduled to begin the trip in Sydney where he was speaking at a banking convention, and then continue on to the Gold Coast to snorkel the Great Barrier Reef and horseback ride through the foothills of Tamborine Mountain.

Anyone else could have seen that this date vacation was not going to end well. Just six weeks before, I'd been dumped by a man I was crazy about. After we dated sporadically for nine months, he'd told me I wasn't relationship material. I was crushed. My Sydney date was, himself, just out of a messy divorce. He still couldn't even utter his wife's name.

Although my date lived in New York, he was completing a special work project near me in Denver, so we'd been out at least seven times already. Everything about him looked great on paper—he was successful, handsome, super intelligent—but there was a catch. We were clearly attracted to each other, but couldn't seem to connect. It was as if our minds and bodies were speaking different languages. From my perspective, our lips just didn't know how to dance together. Kissing him felt like making out with a slab of wood.

Yet against all evidence, I still thought Mr. Wall Street and I had a chance. After so many recent dating fiascos, I just wanted *something* to work out. So when he told me about his trip overseas and invited me to go with him, I accepted. And when he asked me to buy my own plane ticket, although I thought it a bit ungenerous considering his apparent wealth, I agreed.

We got along well on the plane, cuddling together while gazing out the windows at dazzling meteor showers. Arriving in Sydney, we headed to one of the most gorgeous hotels in the South Pacific, the Shangri-La. Aptly named, it towers over Sydney Harbor and has breathtaking views of the Sydney Harbour Bridge and the Sydney Opera House.

But despite these good omens, it soon appeared to me that Mr. Wall Street was suffering from what I call posttraumatic relationship disorder. It has symptoms such as talking constantly about an ex, comparing current relationships and behaviors to past partners, marinating in victim mentality, and feeling paralyzed in new situations due to a fear of recreating past painful experiences. Maybe you have experienced this phenomenon in your own dating partners or in yourself.

To be honest, I had a touch of it too. I was fixating on my own relationship that had just ended. My thoughts kept returning to the passion and magnetic attraction I'd recently shared. This only amplified my focus on the lack of compatibility I was currently experiencing. Being a psychologist only aggravated the situation. I forgot that I was on vacation— on a *date*—and put on my psychologist hat. Breaking my own rule against working while dating, I began to try to "fix" Mr. Wall Street. Yet, as I doled out psychological and spiritual advice, I was becoming increasingly uncomfortable and irritable. If I admit the truth, I was impatient for my date to *change already* so that we could have fun. But I was getting the sense that no amount of discussion was going to relax him. To make things worse, he didn't get my spiritual jargon and was beginning to look at me as some sort of weirdo. It wasn't long until we began to argue, going round and round in unhelpful sparring. I suggested parting ways. He suggested starting over. We were at a standstill.

Within hours, we each managed to find an escape route. I answered an online dating email from an Australian man and went to lunch with him. (How synchronistic that this man had contacted me while I was *in* Sydney!) Mr. Wall Street claimed his father had had a heart attack and that he needed to return to New York immediately. Instead, he secretly stayed in Australia, going on to the Gold Coast by himself (something he revealed to me months later). I continued on alone in Sydney. The other date was a nice distraction, but, as I told that man from the beginning, I was in no way interested in pursuing yet another dating adventure in Sydney. When he heard that news, he graciously escorted me back to the subway so I could return to my hotel.

When I got back to the Shangri-La after my tea date, I ended up huddled in a sad little heap on the bathroom floor, searching for a return flight back to Denver on my laptop. I found that by paying a simple $300 change fee I could be home free. Upon arriving at the bustling Sydney Airport at 7:30 the next morning, I realized that my flight wouldn't leave for hours. I decided to get some breakfast but when I went to pay, it turned out they only took credit cards and mine wouldn't work. Then I wanted to use the pay phone to call the other online date I'd had lunch with and the call wouldn't go through. I went to the ticket counter and they sent me two floors up into the bowels of airport administration. When I got there, I was told that I should "never" be on that floor. By the time I found someone who could potentially change my return ticket, my flight change fee was now up to $850. It was if I faced a giant hand of "NO" everywhere I turned.

Feeling completely exhausted, a little sick and a LOT hungry, I sat down and emphatically stated to Spirit, "Okay I get that all of this is a 'NO.' I'm just going to sit and wait for 'YES.'" I surrendered into the moment at hand and simply waited. That is when I hit rock bottom. I was at the depth of my despair. I thought about the previous twenty-four hours. I'd gone on a date on the other side of the world, paying for it myself! I felt like I was on an endless, unrequited search for love. The amplitude of my dating mayhem revealed itself in its entirety. I was exhausted, sad, and extremely frustrated. I was embarrassed and ashamed of the insanity of my search. I mean, I had even posted this escapade on social media for all to see!

The noisy judgment in my head was threatening to take over. The questions rattled around: *How desperate have you become? To what degree will you allow this search for love, security, and acceptance to overtake your life?* WHAT ARE YOU DOING?!!

I felt hopeless and couldn't fathom how I could possibly fill this seemingly empty void inside me. Most of all, I was scared. I felt utterly alone on the other side of the world, looking for something I could only find within. But as I sat there in the airport, a tiny pinpoint of light began to shine within my heart, almost as if my heart was peeking through all the mind soot and sludge that had settled there. I thought about what was going on for me on the home front. My girls, luckily, were safe and secure back in the states, visiting my mom on vacation in Illinois. So, for just these moments in time, I was technically free from all responsibility. And then, I had a gem of an idea. Maybe I could stay on in Sydney for that same $850 change fee and finish out my date by going out with myself.

Wouldn't that be fun? I mean, there I was in one of the most beautiful metropolitan cultural centers of the world. Maybe I could just settle down and enjoy it a little? My girls were safe and cared for and having fun. Why not rest and wait for my flight back in a few days? So, with that burst of brightness inside me, I hailed a cab back to the city and booked a room for myself in the middle of Sydney. When I opened my new hotel room door, I burst into happy tears. I was taking myself on a date! I was paying for my *own* hotel room! I was in charge of my own happiness. For the next few days I luxuriated in my hotel room and roamed the city on my own inner-city walkabout. I took bubble baths while listening to recordings from the Opera House Symphony Orchestra. I bought myself a new dress and went out for Spanish tapas, watching all the nightlife unfold around me. I sat for hours in the Royal Botanic Garden and took pictures of flower petals. I wandered leisurely through the art museum and took in the paintings. I went to the State Library of New South Wales and read whatever book seemed to fall off the shelf (that day it was a book on English author J.R.R. Tolkien about his inspiration for *The Hobbit*).

A world of mindful living unfolded within me and I felt a bubbling of peace begin to percolate throughout my body. The present moment was at hand. I was feeling alive and deeply focused within myself! Vibrant! Captivated by every sense, every sensation. The salmon and salad I ate for lunch one day seemed to explode with a newness of flavors. In my stillness and presence within the world around me, in the calming down of my seeking, I was beginning to tap into a new way of being. It was as if I had sunk to the quiet bottom of the ocean and all other activity was crashing in the waves so far above me. I had found peace. I had found presence of mind and heart. I had found . . . me.

From that vantage point of stillness and quiet, even in the midst of Sydney, I was able to look at my life objectively. I began to ask myself just what it was that I was expending all my energy searching for. And the only answer that made any sense was love. I wanted love. I wanted to feel cherished, adored, and seen. I wanted to find love notes at my morning coffee, on the windshield of my car, and in my inbox. I wanted to feel safe, secure, and cared for. I wanted to feel as if I mattered so much to someone that I might even be indispensable.

Know what? On my date with myself in Sydney, I had all of that, all of it. *I* was the date I had been waiting for! It was ME! It was my own heart. I wanted love from myself. It felt like the first time I'd ever touched my own heart so deeply. I was having an incredible experience. However, as I got closer to the end of my stay, I felt the worry and stress of everyday life begin to creep back in. *When would I schedule my daughter's orthodontist appointment? When would I set up the roof repair? Could I stay out of debt this month?* I feared this mountain of daily stressors would send me back into a frenzy of online dating to escape the pressure I felt.

I quickly made a pact with myself. I knew I hadn't discovered everything that I wanted to know about this heart glimpse I'd just experienced. So I vowed to stop seeking—no more dating for a while. No more looking for love outside myself until I'd genuinely found it within me. I stood at the window of my hotel room that last night in Sydney and stated loudly, and with feeling—to Spirit, myself, and anyone else who might have been around to hear—that my heart was my new date. I was going to start living my love story. I was going to find it within me. Whatever that meant, I was going to do it. And I was going to start RIGHT NOW! Or . . . maybe right when I got back to the United States, since on the way home I sat next to a charismatic Hollywood writer. But regardless, I was done with dating! *Hear that, me? Done with dating.* And with that vow, Spirit quickly began to help me organize my life in a brand new direction. Though not without tying up some dangling participles first.

Valentine's Day Validation

Several weeks later, it was Valentine's Day. Each year I look forward to this day of romance (I know that's probably hard to believe given the previous content in this chapter). Being a die-hard romantic, I love the *idea* of love.

I had recently returned from Australia with the intention of beginning to source love from inside myself rather than from outside of myself. A new vibration of life was starting to be instilled within me, and Neverland was slowly fading back into the far-off clouds. I could still feel its presence, however—I still had a ways to go to extract myself completely.

Toward the end of my dating in Neverland, I'd foolishly pinned my romantic hopes on two men who'd danced in and out of my life in recent times. One of them was the Salesman, a charming and elusive guy on whom I'd passed three years of my life negotiating a romance—and then a friendship and a business partnership. A week earlier, he'd emailed looking for an answer to his request for an additional investment in a business vision. I admit that I had originally loaned him a little money in the hopes that I could pin down his love and keep his affection—there was that seeking behavior again. But now it was time to draw a clear boundary, one that I had struggled to maintain throughout our associations.

On the night of February 13, I had been struggling to sleep, fighting a nagging fear that if I loaned him even more money to fund yet more business ventures, he wouldn't pay back what he already owed me. Finally, I sent him a middle-of-the-night message asking about my earlier loan to him. I opened his response at work the next morning. Instead of answering my question, he evaded. His reply was a long-winded excuse. One phrase stood out. It said: "I see no path forward on a personal or professional level."

Upon reading those words, my heart did a sickening nosedive. I started obsessing, clinging to the past, and wanting him (and me) to be able to show up and be adults, to take care of the finances and to take care of our relationship. I was angry with myself for not accepting that none of this was happening. I'd had a closer relationship with him than with any other man in Neverland. And yet, I questioned myself; *if your closest relationship was with someone who could so easily cast you aside, then how close was it, really?* Maybe he was just charming and I had been fooled.

Suddenly, I felt the pain from previous times I'd been walked out on. My limbic system—the part of the brain in charge of emotions—went into high gear. Then, after the shock faded, I was furious. Once again, I had fallen for this trick. I had fallen for a rejecting man, and this one had already rejected me before! What's worse, I had made myself a perfect target for him.

I told my boss I was suddenly sick, went home, and crawled into bed to lick my wounds. Two hours later, still consumed by sadness and anger, I checked my email again. To my immense excitement, there was a message from the New York Cowboy, a man whom I'd been seeing on and off for nine months. Although he lived in a town near mine, he worked all over the country, was often in New York, and he loved horses, so I had dubbed him the New York Cowboy.

Our latest break had been three months and he'd answered my emails only sporadically. From the beginning, our whirlwind affair was based on attraction rather than commitment; he was clear that he didn't want a relationship. However, I clung to every possible hint that his heart might be changing. I was lost in fantasyland and so blinded by my desire that I didn't even notice in reality, he just wanted to play.

Despite all the signs, when I saw his email in my inbox, my broken heart picked itself up and dipped right back into the fantasy, hoping to avoid feeling the pain of rejection I'd felt earlier in the morning. Maybe this Valentine's Day could be redeemed after all! The email came on this auspicious day of love! I whispered to that waiting email message, "Oh, there you are!" and clicked to open it.

After a brief hello, the email read, "Perhaps most significantly, I met a woman in the last couple of months . . . and am not stretching to say . . . have literally fallen in love with her. Certainly a contributor to my email inattentiveness, but such a wonderful addition to my life." Wow. I stared at the screen in disbelief, my heart plummeting again. Really? And, by the way, he continued, I should retrieve the books I'd lent him from his mail box, because he was traveling.

Just like that, my association with these two men evaporated into the ether. I put my head down and cried. *What kind of woman gets a Valentine's Day like this?* I thought, miserably. *A totally unlovable, desperate woman who attracts utterly thoughtless men who send thoughtless emails. Seriously?*

A Jewel song, "Foolish Games," began to play in my head. The song struck me. I had played all these foolish games with these men and now I was expecting them to see that my heart was "bleeding before them." I had some sort of expectation that they would care about how I felt in this moment. But these emails showed that my heart was the least of their considerations. All along, in my desperate search for love outside myself, I had clung to the hope that at some point these men would begin to care more deeply.

In my delusion, and despite all the evidence, I thought they would change. All arrows had been pointing to the fact that they were deeply unavailable or simply not inclined to change, but I wasn't accepting reality.

That's when it hit me. I was singing Jewel's song to myself and no one else. I had been forgetting to live my love story with me. I was the one playing foolish games by choosing to tear myself apart over these men who never really wanted me in the first place. They were just helping me to see that I was the responsible party. I was forgetting my inner Shangri-La, the Shangri-Love, that I'd touched in Sydney—that I was living my love story with *me* now, not with unavailable men.

I paused. I remembered that I had rededicated myself to my own heart, to listening deeply to my soul. First, I let go of my black/white thinking that said the Salesman and the New York Cowboy were *wrong* and that this situation was *bad*. Next, I remembered that I didn't have all the answers. I couldn't possibly know everything about this situation and how it was linked to everything else in life. And I took a deep breath and turned within to listen to the thoughts that were swirling around in my head. Whew! There were a lot of them. I kept remembering all the times men had walked out on me. I'd always thought of the emails as rejection letters. I watched these thoughts for a while, and gave myself permission to let go of my countless stories of rejection and abandonment, pausing to simply feel and breathe. I completely surrendered to the feelings. Once I left the stories behind, the emotions felt suddenly purer, less intense. They flowed quickly past.

While in quiet contemplation, I guided myself in a meditation in which I saw my heart energy swirling above the situation, and I was able to view it from afar. Soon, alternative thoughts began to enter my mind. I asked myself, *What are some alternative ways to think about the Valentine's Day emails?* And listened to the thoughts bounce around in my mind like Ping Pong balls. In cutting ties with me, maybe these two men were sending me validations rather than valentines, validation that I was ready to cease looking for a relationship outside myself and begin to have one with me.

Maybe this marked the start of a period where I would associate with others, especially men, who were interested in genuine connection, authentic communication, and taking responsibility for oneself. Maybe I didn't quite know the ultimate purpose of receiving these emails, but could decide in the moment to interpret them in a way that supported loving myself. Were these messages simply reminders that the Salesman and the New York Cowboy were not aligned with where I was in that moment? Maybe where they were was just *different* from where I was, and there was nothing wrong with that. Maybe these emails were actually gifts that came from the newness of loving myself, which I had been practicing these past few months. Maybe I was creating this situation exactly as it was unfolding.

With those thoughts, peace swept over me. This was my chance to practice thinking something new and different. It was my chance to interpret things in a way that worked for me. I could shine brighter and not hit the dimmer switch. Gosh, if I was living my love story *with me*, then it was the perfect time to send myself the kinds of valentines that I wanted. This was my chance to fill the day with good feelings and good thoughts, putting into them *exactly* what I wanted to receive and to feel. I knew from brain science that repeating new thoughts over time would establish a new pattern of thoughts in my brain, thoughts that would become automatic if I rehearsed them over time. It was time to start rehearsing these new thoughts!

I began to contemplate all the things that I liked about living my love story with me.

- I liked that I got to spend quality time getting to know myself better.

- I liked that I was beginning to set healthy boundaries about lending money to friends.

- I liked that I was stating my true thoughts and desires instead of keeping them to myself for fear of rejection.

- I liked that I was not rejecting myself in this moment and that I was celebrating my decision to state my truth.

- I liked that I was turning my thoughts around so that I would feel better.

In thinking all these thoughts, I knew it was time to turn my day around.

I closed my email, put away the laptop, and got out of bed. I texted my daughter, Maiya, at school and thirty minutes later whisked her away for a lunch at the best Vietnamese place in town. We ordered yummy spring rolls and toasted our favorite things in life with iced mint tea. My daughter, then fourteen, was eagerly planning our Valentine's Day dinner for her friends that night. She had already found the perfect heart-shaped cherry cheesecake. We celebrated Valentine's Day together.

That Valentine's Day fully catapulted me into research mode. What would it mean to find my heart? What would it mean to live my love story with me? When would I start to hear my heart whispering more often in my ear? Why didn't I feel love oozing out from all around me since I'd made the decision to turn my love inward? The journey to awaken my heart and begin loving myself was just beginning. I was super anxious, but still completely devoted to the task. I wanted to find that love that I'd just barely touched in Sydney. The biggest question for me was where and how to start.

CHAPTER 2:

A CRACK IN THE ARMOR

Stopping dating wasn't the easiest thing I'd ever done. And to be honest, that part of my life didn't die the moment I set the intention. It sort of petered out over a series of several months and a few really nightmarish outings. These dates were becoming increasingly useless since I'd already put one foot out the door. Finally, I did lose interest in even my lukewarm attempts at dating and it all came to a halt. I took down all my profiles on the various Internet sites, stopped going to parties, and no longer called my friends to report the play-by-plays of my dating drama. I sat down with me, myself (and, of course, my daughters because I continued to find immense joy in parenting).

It was really, really quiet. I mean, imagine always being surrounded by music, some of it loud and obnoxious, some a polka at the circus, and some a gentle ballet through the forest, and suddenly it stops. Silence. No notes. No dancing. My texting screen went dark. My email inbox had no daily catalogue of the latest available men. Just . . . stillness. For the first time I could begin to hear and feel what had been going on behind the music. I'd thought I would immediately fall madly in love with myself, beginning to live my own epic love story with me, (and I would become enraptured with being alone with myself, kind of like my experience in Sydney, but more permanent). But in reality, what I was feeling was anxiety—pure, unadulterated anxiety. It was an inner whirlwind of discomfort mixed with a distinct feeling of numbness; I felt frozen in place.

Then came the urge to wiggle, to seek out a prince to ride off with into another sunset. I had a desperate desire to take up my usual distractions—it was almost more than I could bear at times. Until this moment of stopping and pausing, I hadn't been aware of my addiction to love and my dependency on others for my happiness, well-being, and sense of love.

My Well-Fortified Heart

But now that I'd stopped, I could step back and take a bird's-eye view of my story until this point in time. What I saw looked like a princess in a tall, dark, prison tower, a princess (me) who'd been attempting to escape imprisonment in the tower for as long as I could remember. All those princes had answered the calls to join me. Some dropped in for a quick visit, others stayed for a while. Each prince found a different me when he arrived; I was whomever he wanted me to be. Some encountered a brainless doll. Others discovered a bohemian dancer, a delicate fairy, a spiritual teacher, a loving mother, or an ice queen. Several princes leapt from the tower, running to freedom in the woods. A handful of others appeared to be thrown out, landing in a heap of brokenhearted tears. After each exit, I would sit down and cry. I felt waves of frustration, sadness, and anger, and couldn't quite put my finger on what was going on.

From my bird's-eye view, I could see that the roles I'd taken on were ones that would most suit each respective prince; I had tried to adapt to his energy. It was exhausting work! And, regardless, either I was pushing toward him or pulling away from him, and vice versa on his part. True connection and intimacy were always just beyond arm's reach. I had the stark realization that, after all these years, I didn't have a clue as to my true colors, my true form, my authentic heart, or even what I was searching so desperately for.

Very "Special" Relationships

A Course in Miracles, the spiritual guide by Helen Schucman, defines the sort of relationships I was experiencing as "special." Not special in the sense that they were wonderful treasures of love, but special in the sense that they were ego-driven, saturated in judgment, and intent on separation rather than unification. There was no connection, no cherishing of the Divine within my partner and me. Instead, there was competition and figuring out what one could "get" from the other, a search for joy based in external circumstances. When the man I was dating was meeting my "needs," I was happy; when he wasn't, I was devastated. It was like an eternal yo-yo in and out of hell. Never satisfied, I was totally dependent on the various dating outcomes and interactions for my overall sense of fulfillment.

A *Course in Miracles* further states, "To believe that **special** relationships, with **special** love, can offer you salvation is the belief that separation is salvation." My salvation was certainly not in these dating adventures—that I knew for sure. Where my salvation was, I wasn't yet certain; it would take a deeper look at what exactly was going on while I was in Neverland.

Mirror, Mirror, on the Wall

Quieting down and hitting the pause button gave me the chance to look in the mirror. While gazing at my reflection, I imagined myself swathed in suits of armor that I, the princess, had been using as a defense mechanism to distance myself from others. First, there was the suit of "judgment armor" that I used to either be better than or worse than my partner. It was ugly and heavy, teetering and swaying as I walked. Another suit of armor was my sense of humor. Just when things would start to approximate a more genuine place in relationship, I would crack a joke, or laugh something off, keeping a more connected, present moment at bay. Still another suit of armor was conflict, used to create distance. If things were beginning to smooth out and sail straight into comfort, I would pick a fight, stirring up stormy seas to retain a sense of what I felt was "normal." Even though all the suits of armor were weighing heavily on me, I didn't know anything different and didn't have the conscious tools to shift the relationship into a more genuine, heart-based place. The armor was mostly part of my subconscious, so even though I detested donning it, I wasn't consciously aware of how to rid myself of it just yet.

As I continued to look closely at my reflection, facing myself in a present way, I felt lonely, isolated, and completely void of the ability to establish deep connections with others, especially in romance. How had it all come to be? I began to contemplate my defense mechanisms, not from a place of blame, but from a place of insight. The Persian mystic poet Rumi wrote, "Everything in the universe is within you. Ask all from yourself." This is what I was prepared to do, to look inside until I found clarity. From where had I started putting on the armors? As with most of us, I began to see that I had learned these modes of protection in childhood. And looking back, I wouldn't trade one moment of these opportunities for learning because they catapulted my spiritual journey into love. Peering through the challenge, I can now see the inherent gift of each one.

Enchantment on the Farm

I grew up in a world ripe with imagination. On my family's little farm in Illinois, we lived in a huge farmhouse surrounded by barns and went for daily romps in our own forest. All through my childhood, my sister and I were immersed in fodder for play.

My father was a scientist/engineer and my mother was a musician/housewife/biology major. Because of their diverse interests, our house was filled with engaging eccentricities. Our playroom was loaded to the ceiling with toys and wonders. The house, which was built in the late 1800s, had many nooks and crannies in which fantasy was waiting to be born. I could crawl into a closet and make it my treehouse; the phone became a wise owl. The days were filled with gardening, walks in the forest, and bike rides with monarch butterflies as our guides. We hunted mushrooms and pressed wildflowers. At night, the crickets' song would lull me to sleep and I would wake to the sound of distant cows mooing and birds chirping. Sometimes I would head into the woods toting homemade cornbread and play as if I were traveling via wagon train on the Oregon Trail.

Despite all this gorgeous wonder, these years were also filled with average dysfunction. It wasn't deep, wounding trauma, but more like a slow leak in the area of emotional presence. My mom struggled sometimes with depression and my dad was somewhat emotionally unavailable. Over time, my interactions with my family led me to question my own worthiness. This questioning began to interfere with my ability to receive and give love.

My parents, who were high school sweethearts, eventually separated just weeks after I entered high school. That was where the chapter of my childhood enchantment ended. My dad took a job in a town a couple of hours away, and my mom, sister, and I moved out of our lovely farm and into a tiny house that my grandparents owned. It was technically in the same town, but miles from what I considered my home. The divorce and move left me distraught; I felt like a fish flopping out of water. I was just starting high school and, being in the sensitive years where peer opinion was paramount, I was ashamed that I was now from a "divorced family." In our close-knit, highly religious community, it seemed like I was now a "sinner." And I missed my dad dreadfully. While he and I didn't have an especially expressive relationship, I often sought refuge in our intellectual discussions and thrived on the attention he gave me for being "smart." He was funny too, and I missed his absurdities, like when he spilled a glass of milk on the table at dinner and then proceeded to lap it up off the table like a puppy, sending me into uncontrollable giggles.

My response to this new situation was to get a boyfriend whose family life I admired, attempting to fill the ever-increasing void within myself. This boyfriend, a dear, dear friend, was with me throughout high school. Meanwhile, I felt like my own family evaporated almost entirely. The few bits left were steeped in so much sadness.

CHINKS IN THE ARMOR

As I continued to self-reflect, I thought about how I'd interacted with my parents while growing up. How much I'd sought their attention, both before and after the divorce. Looking back, I knew it had been my way of trying to avoid nagging fears of rejection and abandonment. But alas, I couldn't get around these fears, so to compensate, I developed multiple ways to protect myself, including:

- Pleasing others to get love.

- Focusing on others instead of myself.

- Stifling my voice until I would erupt in emotional outburst.

- Rehearsing thoughts, such as *I'm not loveable; I'm not worthy; I'm all alone; People abandon me, especially when I am "real"; I'm too emotional; I'm shut down; I'm too scared.*

The quiet period after I stopped dating allowed me the time to finally realize and acknowledge these defense mechanisms. My first instinct was to vanquish them. I had an anger-fueled determination to stop pleasing others, to turn the focus on myself, to share my opinion at every turn, and to think only positive thoughts! But I also felt a huge sadness in having acted that way all these years. The sadness then turned into something else . . . more like fear. Despite the pain at having behaved in so many stunted ways, I was terrified of what would happen if I left it all behind for good! I was scared because I thought it was keeping me "safe" from rejection and abandonment. In reality, though, all I was doing was rejecting and abandoning myself. *I was maintaining the pain!* I realized that it was going to take more than just sheer will to get rid of my defenses.

LOVE IN BUBBLE BATHS

Because I was so unaccustomed to stopping and being still, I was restless at first. I wanted some answers. What did this process of finding my heart entail? What did it mean? The first thing I thought was that it was probably about practicing self-love. Since books are a source of happiness and information for me, I turned to them. I bought *a lot* of books on self-love. And I got busy loving myself. In the midst of taping little notes to my mirror, reciting love mantras while taking bubble baths, and getting massages and more sleep, I still felt a little perplexed. I didn't get that I was mistaking—as were many of the books I'd bought—self-care for self-love. I gained an important step in practicing self-care, but I was still mentally marinating on love rather than feeling much of it.

There is a well-known Sioux saying that says, "The longest journey you will make in your life is from your head to your heart." I believed it! That's what it felt like. Securely stationed in my head and reluctant to leave there, all my attempts at trying to feel better were landing me securely in a state of uneasiness. Even in the midst of activating a new level of self-care, I could still feel the constant buzz of angst underneath it all. It was a steady unease, a sense of being uncomfortable in my own skin. Bubble baths weren't cutting it. With all this calm and quiet and time for self-reflection, I wasn't headed toward more peace, the kind I had touched in Sydney; I was stirring up a flurry of mess within myself, a torrent of feelings that had been stuffed down for so long. Anger flooded in and quickly behind that, sadness. Next, I felt an elixir of anxiety and fear. Finally, loneliness, a deep sense of being totally alone.

THE SACRED HEART VOW

One of my favorite quotes is from the book *Unattended Sorrow* by Stephen Levine: "Healing, then, becomes not the absence of pain but the increased ability to meet it with mercy instead of loathing." Laying down the armor of my defenses was going to be a slow process. Just as it had taken years of fear to acquire this armor, it would take time and love to dismantle it. I knew that behind it was my own heart. I was going to shift my desire to stage a quick and definitive "demolition" to a slow melting of the metal. Love would be my guide. Love would be the power that would melt my armors of protection.

What would it mean for love to be my guide? I would stop looking outside myself for validation and love and begin to turn within in earnest. Up until that point, I'd been trying to find and extract love externally. I could now clearly see that my romantic relationships had been devoid of genuine compassion or connection. I was now ready to follow that deep yearning of my soul, that essence of Shangri-Love that I had discovered while in Sydney.

While getting in touch with my heart, I recognized that I could no longer find sustaining joy in the more superficial nature of romantic love, career success, material stuff, or any other "god" of the physical world. These things weren't "wrong" or "bad"; it was just that I was no longer going to make them my source of fulfillment and love. I wanted to experience a deeper love, the love of my soul, the love of Spirit or God. This process came with an invitation to deeper awareness, more capacity to feel and a connection to my own divine nature. I had forgotten that I was in partnership with the Divine, that I was made of the same fabric that stitches together the universe.

All this brought to mind a time a few years prior when I sang backup for a kirtan band one New Year's Eve. Kirtan, if you aren't familiar with the term, is call-and-response devotional chanting from India. Usually chants are composed of Sanskrit words, although performers in the West have infused English verse into the songs. The words carry the power and energy of ancient wisdom, love, and devotion. Just think: thousands of years of chanting! The meaning and energy in the words have been embossed, imbued, and imprinted within them. The first time I chanted at a kirtan, it sounded to me like they were singing the words "chicken soup," but I was deeply moved by the sound and energy even though I had no clue what was being sung. The mere recitation of the syllables and immersion in the event had an effect on me. Ever since, chanting has been a part of my spiritual practice. That New Year's Eve kirtan, the band, and we in the audience wrote and created sankalpas. These sankalpas, which in Sanskrit means solemn vows of the heart, carried forth our sacred intentions.

Faced with the task of diving in to find my heart and learning a deeper meaning of love, I decided to create a sankalpa to guide and support me on my journey. A sankalpa is a collaboration between God and your will. (Or the Divine and your will, or Spirit and your will—whatever higher power feels right to you.) At this moment, I actually got down on my knees, feeling so weary from my epic searching and protecting, and dedicated my intention to God. This is, in essence, what I said:

I vow to find and feel my heart.

I vow to clear all that is in the way of my connection with my heart.

I vow to awaken my heart energies so they may guide my life.

I vow to make peace with love.

THE ULTIMATE SURRENDER

With my sankalpa, I felt a part of myself surrender and relax. It was like I was finally ready to let go of the search, to let go of the endless attempt to find love. *What if I am just here in this moment, here right now?* I thought. *I know, I know, all the spiritual teachers say to be here now, but I don't think I've ever really tried it for any extended period of time. What if I were to really trust that God has got this? What would happen if I hit the pause button on my life for an extended amount of time?* These were the things I asked myself.

One thing I knew for sure: it was time to stop protecting my heart. It was time to stop forcing life to meet my demands for love. I was aware on some level that my notion of love was utterly skewed. What if I allowed life to show me what the nature of love *is*? Michael A. Singer raises a question about this concept in his book, *The Surrender Experiment*, asking,

> "Am I better off making up an alternate reality in my mind and then fighting with reality to make it be my way, or am I better off letting go of what I want and serving the same forces of reality that managed to create the entire perfection of the universe around me?"

Well, when he put it that way, I chose the latter. He goes on to explain that surrendering is not about dropping out of life but about leaping into life: really stepping into a place where, instead of putting your own fears and desires in the cockpit, you let your heart fly your life plane.

What would this look like, exactly? Well, for one thing, it meant that I would trust in the flow of life to bring me true love instead of trying to will it into existence. Did this mean I could never go on an online date again? No, but it did mean that I needed to find peace within myself in order to be a good partner to someone, instead of looking to that partner to give me peace.

What I wanted was to experience the genuine nature of love, a real Shangri-Love where love was a presence and not a feeling. When I was truly ultra-present with myself in Sydney, I had felt love as a state of being, a sense of peace within my heart. I wanted that sort of presence of love. I called it Shangri-Love because it was like being in a paradise within my heart. When I was in that space, all was peaceful, all was okay with my world and I was saturated in a simple grace of well-being. It was as if in that place, in the stillness of my heart, all was aligned. I was part of a greater whole, part of God.

A Glimpse beyond the Drama

It was all set. I was going to "be in my heart"—I was ready. There was just one problem: when I started the process, when I turned to focus on my heart, it seemed like a desolate place. I'd had a powerful, undeniable connection to my heart in Sidney, but back home, when I tried to reconnect, I felt . . . nothing. Numbness. I drew a blank. I didn't feel anything when I looked inside. The natural questions arose – *What do I really want? What is the nature of the real me? What am I looking for?* – but I was met with a deafening silence. You could have heard a pin drop in this vastness, the size of Mongolia.

There was silence, but for brief moments I would catch a glimpse of myself from outside the story of my life. This was a different experience for me. Sure, I'd taken the "bird's-eye view" before, but this time I felt even more distance, like I could not only see but *understand* what was going on. I was acting as a sort of voyeur of my own life, like I was separated from it. In these periods of time when I was not immersed in the story of myself, I actually began to feel peace. Dr. Thomas Hora writes about this in his book, *Beyond the Dream*, in which he talks about the "transcendent observer."

One day as I was journaling, I had another one of those moments, where I literally could see my life as a story (one that, up to this point, rather resembled *Days of Our Lives*), and an image of a flowing river popped into my mind. As I considered this concept, I put down the pen and held one hand behind my head just above my right ear. This was my "observer" hand. The other hand I moved in front of me like a river, making a swimming motion like waves. These waves were the ever-changing flow of my life, the "neverending story." My observer, on the other hand (pun intended), was constant and unwavering. This observer was my eternal essence, my heart, my spirit, the part of me that doesn't change regardless of the circumstances of my life. It doesn't change, it doesn't move, it just IS.

That moment, as insignificant as it might seem, changed my life. I felt the power within me that came when I saw myself as the observer and not the endless drama. If I could get enough space between my story and me, then I would have the power to change it. When I wasn't fully ensconced in the story, perceiving it as *me*, then I could identify more with my essence. This was exciting!

What I didn't know yet was that stopping my dating spree, activating my newfound observer, and staying present with what was going on within me, would lead me more deeply into the fire of hidden emotions that had prompted the dating in the first place. Nothing was "wrong" with this pain. In fact, I sensed it could be my rite of passage into a new way of being. But, would I be able to stay the course and feel the heat for long enough to get back to the state of peace I'd found in Sydney? Life after Neverland was presently gearing up to be a bit heated. I was determined not to sugarcoat, rose petal, or disguise my pain in any way. The pain of dependence and seeking love outside me far outweighed this current pain of transition. I would not go back. I'd allow this present "ick" to propel me forward. I would forge ahead, deeper into my feelings of discomfort, deeper into the fire of my strong emotions. It was time to feel the burn. I prayed for the staying power to truly transform.

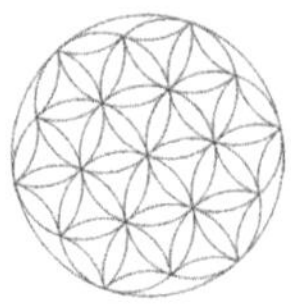

Shangri-Love Activity:
DEVELOP YOUR OWN SACRED HEART VOW

Close your eyes and place your hands over your heart. Breathe in gently through your nose and release the breath through your mouth. Repeat several times. Imagine that you are breathing in and out through your heart space. Sit in stillness a few moments and listen within yourself. Allow the thoughts to flow with simple awareness and no judgment.

As you sit in this peaceful state, tune in to your present longings—what you desire to create in your life. Ask yourself these questions:

> "What are my next steps in connecting more deeply with my heart?"

> "What do I most want to embody in my life and to experience right now?"

> "What is the highest demonstration of love in my life in this moment?"

> "What does love want to express through me in my life now?"

Listen and breathe. Allow whatever comes to you to be. Accept the Divine guidance with love. Ask grace to speak to you in ways that you understand. When you feel complete you can open your eyes.

Now, use whatever answers entered your mind to create your sacred heart vows and record them in a journal. Form your sentences beginning with "I vow to . . . ." When you are done writing your vows, finish your session by stating out loud, holding your journal over your heart, "I surrender these sacred heart vows in sacred trust. Love guides my life for the greatest good, and I release these words with deep faith and love. And so it is."

Celebrate your vows. Dance, sing, chant, pray, and saturate these words in devotion and reverence, whatever that means for you. Place these words in a sacred place where you can read them and hold them in love every day. You can repeat this process again and again as love flows into and through your life.

CHAPTER 3:

INTO THE FIRE

The fire of suffering becomes the light of consciousness.
~Eckhart Tolle

When I put a stop to the habitual ways that I'd used relationships to provide entertainment, validation, and a sense of safety, I began to feel some raw pain in their absence. As often happens when the distraction from one's underlying feelings is no longer available, I was able to finally experience the emotional landscape that I'd been trying so hard to avoid. But I could sense that if I stayed and faced the feelings, then I could find that peace that I had a taste of in Australia. The first pains were about feeling abandoned and totally alone. Even though I had my beautiful girls around me and friends and work colleagues, etc., I felt like I was on a deserted island—small, helpless, sad, and so insignificant.

Luckily, my observer—the unchangeable part of me that is my heart and my spirit—was activated enough that I didn't collapse fully back into that story, but it wasn't without pain that I was beginning to look at my life and take full responsibility for everything in it. Thoughts of "he/she should have . . . " rose up again and again, but in activating my observer, I was able to watch them rise, try to take over, and then slowly fall back down again.

My observer was keeping me on track, and yet my mind was confused. The food that had been my sustenance for so many years was no longer nourishing, and what's more, it was downright poison to my spiritual development and ability to be a whole, joyful being.

Changing habitual thought patterns after a lifetime of use actually creates biochemical changes in the body. Sometimes my emotional responses from stopping dating were so intense, I couldn't even think straight, and, if I wasn't careful, I would spiral into feelings of panic. Thinking straight is a function of the frontal lobe in the brain, that part of the prefrontal cortex that sits right in the front, behind the forehead. Dr. Joe Dispenza, in his book *Evolve Your Brain*, states, "The biggest reason most people cannot utilize the frontal lobe is because we are addicted to our emotions and feelings from the body." This was my experience. Stopping doing the thing that was sustaining a sense of well-being in my life, albeit poorly, brought forth an entourage of uncomfortable sensations. I realized, however, as I read further into Dr. Dispenza's book, that if I stayed with these sensations without falling back into the previous behaviors or engaging in new distracting behaviors, then they would die out over time. I was going to have to feel the burn of these emotions in order to begin to build new, more empowering ways of thought and new ways of being in my world.

I once saw an interview with the spiritual teacher Adyashanti, in which he was sharing the story of how he'd gone to the hospital after breaking something—maybe his finger or arm—and while he was sitting there in pain, waiting for treatment, he was watching his thoughts. He noted how a challenging thought would rise up in his mind and try to take over his thoughts and feelings. But he'd engaged his inner observer, so the more he watched, the more the thoughts would just rise up partway, and, not having his attention, fall back down into peace. The more he watched, the closer he got to feeling just peace, and eventually he regained his center and felt peaceful. This was my experience in these first few months. I would watch old ways of acting and thinking rise up, and I would remind myself about my inner observer and simply watch my life like I was watching a fairly good dramatic movie. Sometimes my actions would slip up in response to the thoughts—for instance, I would call an old boyfriend and share with him my loneliness, in hopes he would feel compelled to meet up with me. But when this happened I treated it as an opportunity to exercise compassion for myself and use that compassion as the balm to return me to center. This was a tool I practiced again and again in the face of these times of falling down and getting back up. This building-a-relationship-with-me was really tough.

THE SCREAMING CHILD

About the time when I was working on staying in touch with my observer, a friend mentioned some inner child work that she was doing, so I decided to check it out. I found a coach who specialized in this practice and began weekly sessions. When I first looked within to meet my inner child, I didn't like her much. She was unhappy. She had behaviors that I found irritating, such as being whiny, clingy, needy, and scared . . . high maintenance. I experienced something a little like disgust when I first tried to talk with her in meditation. But each week I continued to show up and my coach would guide me to go within, meet her, love her, hold her, and let her know that I was going to care for her. She was different ages at different times, varying from about four to twelve.

Little by little over time, as I journaled with her and communicated over and over, I began to feel more comfortable meeting her. I got to the point where I could look her in the eyes and genuinely enjoy her! The more I paid attention to giving her the attention she needed, the more she transformed into a smiling, energetic, joyful little girl. She delighted in the activities I provided and loved the inner sanctuary I created, especially a treehouse with a wooden swing hanging from the branches, with fireflies all around in the evening. She loved painting, dancing, singing, and sleeping in mountains of feathers or rose petals.

Even though I started to like my inner child much better, she would still surface in my adult life from time to time and take over during an argument. I came to realize that she'd been involved over the years in all my relationships with men. She was the one who felt the need to beg, plead, convince, cling, and manipulate for attention. She was the one who felt so scared and unsure of herself. When she didn't get the attention she wanted or things didn't go her way, she'd throw huge hissy fits.

As she began to get more and more attention from me, she gradually became more happy and playful. I continued this inner child and reparenting work for over a year. I completed a wonderfully freeing, inner-child journey at my spiritual center. At first it seemed like she was throwing bigger fits as a result of being "found out." But as I calmly returned again and again to meet her with compassion and care, she started to calm down. The first effect I noticed was that I wasn't calling every one of my friends to report every instance of drama in my life. The second effect was that I wasn't asking for more attention over social media. And a third effect was that all these behaviors were being replaced with the ability to self-soothe when things didn't go as planned in my life, or at least to bounce back and return to my center more quickly.

An example of this occurred one day in March when I attempted to take my daughters on a hike in the backwoods. We drove an hour into the mountains west of Denver to arrive at a trailhead fifteen minutes from the nearest town. Although it was mid-March, it was a balmy 60 degrees and I figured that since I had a 4x4 SUV, we could invincibly drive through the melting snow. I was wrong. We drove about ten feet and sank into the slushy melt up to the body of the car. The wheels were entirely immersed in slushy, packed, heavy, melting snow. No matter what we tried, the wheels wouldn't budge. We packed rocks underneath the tires. We tried to dig out around it (using a clipboard since that was the only hard object I found in the back of the vehicle). After an hour of exhausting work, we hadn't accomplished a thing. The SUV was there to stay for the time being. Sitting in the bright sun, the girls looked a bit worried.

Although I was somewhat worried myself since we were the only ones out there, I decided to make the best of a difficult situation. I had no cell service, so we walked a mile down the hill to a house and asked to borrow the phone to call a towing company.

Once we'd talked to a tow service and they'd assured us that they would arrive soon, we walked back up the hill to make snow angels and snowmen in the melting mush. We giggled, shared a banana, and made the best of our predicament. At one point, I found the situation so hilariously strange that I couldn't stop laughing. The girls still talk about this fiasco, one of many adventures, to this day. What I noticed during this unexpected bump in the road was that the panic that I used to feel at the onset of a surprise challenge was lessening. I was more able to center my thoughts, to come up with potential solutions, to self-soothe by reassuring myself, to take care of myself by remembering to breathe and pray, and to make the best of the situation in the meantime. I attributed this to my present work with my inner child. She wasn't feeling as ignored, chastised, or sad, which gave the adult me more room to show up and be present in my current life.

After the car incident, I thought I was on my way to getting my inner child under total control. But then something happened that made me feel like I'd digressed. During a devastating and painful argument with an ex-boyfriend I ran, screaming child in tow, to my voice dialogue coach, another professional specializing in inner child work. She calmly listened to my despair and then suggested that the wounded child would never be healed completely. This was both a revelation and a relief! I'd been trying and trying to eradicate all her wounds and to heal her, restoring her to health, rather than allowing her to be just as she was.

As much as I needed to accept her, however, I needed healthy boundaries. My coach suggested that my interior life was like a solar system—my heart was the sun and my inner child was one of the planets. Each had its own gravitational pull. My job as an adult was to use my tools to navigate the space. Then she said something that made me laugh and really hit home at the same time: "Honey, you do not have the luxury any more of spending time on the wounded child planet!"

What did it mean to live on this planet? If I heard my inner child saying things like: *I'm all alone. No one loves me, I'm not loveable, I don't know how to love, I need attention, or I need someone else to make me feel better,* I would go on high alert. I started to notice that these thoughts would bring feelings of despair, sadness, anger, and remorse, so when they came, I would immediately use a tool to move away from that place.

While I was becoming more balanced in this area, my work on it needed to be ongoing, so with the encouragement of my coach, I resolved to meditate with my inner child. The idea was to find a special place for my little wounded girl, get her surrounded by love and then put up some form of protection around her so that she would stay safely in her "love bubble."

When I got my butt on the meditation cushion and closed my eyes, I immediately saw a beautiful, giant oak tree with sweet tiny lights in the branches. There was a wooden swing suspended by ropes, and flowers grew in every corner of the secluded garden. Beneath the tree were huge soft cushions scattered in a pile on the ground. There were gauzy curtains of ruby red, forest green, royal violet, and white that blew gently in the breeze. A partial stone wall surrounded the garden. It felt like a sanctuary to me. I invited my inner little girl to rest there and gave her a huge canvas to paint. She was delighted!

Next came the unconditional love part. Arriving at this part of the meditation and attempting to conjure up a sense of deep, protected, unchanging love, I struggled. I drew a blank. In that moment I wasn't sure if I knew what that kind of love felt like. So I asked myself, who represents this kind of love for me in the spiritual realm? I immediately thought of Kwan Yin, goddess of compassion; Mary, mother of Jesus; and Mother Earth. So I invited them in to hold my little girl, like surrogate mothers. I asked each of them if they would please hold her until I built the unconditional love within myself to have her saturated with that love from me. I felt so filled with gratitude as I saw them there holding my little girl.

To create some sort of protection all around her, I tried putting up a wall. Nope, felt too suffocating. Then, I installed military tanks and guards. Nope, that was too forceful and scary. Finally, I thought of the lightsabers from *Star Wars*. I chose them! Transparent wands of light. That felt good! I left them there.

Coming out of the meditation, I could feel my inner little girl was happy and well cared for. In the coming months, as I felt the navigational pull of her planet, I would check in, mentally visualizing her under her tree in the sanctuary. I also got to know her better, discovering that she had many interests. I sent her rock bands to play along with, a huge cuddly tame tiger to cuddle, giant blue butterflies to dance with, and other various forms of entertainment. I always waited to see the look of delight upon her face and to make sure that the force field had no holes in it. Fairly soon, I was feeling a lot less reactive in arguments and much more calm when I was alone.

I continue to use this technique to this day. When I start to feel an old pattern surface in my mind, I immediately go inside and check on my little girl. I make sure she is safe, cared for, and protected, and, if I am feeling off center, I ask one of the spiritual "mothers" to take over until I feel stronger.

THE PHOENIX FROM THE ASHES

It's been my experience that when I get a new tool to work with, such as meditating with my inner child, Spirit soon brings me the perfect opportunity to practice using the tool. I'm going to share with you a story of *real* fire because it illustrates clearly the feelings and processes I was beginning to practice as I ceased chasing love outside myself and began to look inside to really pay attention to what was going on within me.

One Friday at 5 pm I was driving when a call came in from an unknown number through my car's Bluetooth. An officer, announcing himself as an investigator with the Jefferson County Fire Department said, "Ms. Jazwierska? Are you the owner of the property at 253 Holman Way?" It was the address of a townhome I owned and rented out in a town an hour away. When I confirmed, he went on to say, "I am calling because there has been a serious fire at the property.

We had to enter in through the roof and all the windows are removed. We have finally extinguished it but there is extensive damage. No one was home at the time and no one in the neighboring townhomes was hurt. We are stabilizing the scene and boarding up all the windows and doors as we speak. Don't come down here, there is really nothing you can do. I will call you with more information once the investigation has determined the cause." I awkwardly stuttered a few questions, but the investigator said there wasn't much information he could share at that point. With that, the call was complete.

I pulled into my driveway at home, sat in silence in the car, and stared at my phone. This had been my post-divorce condo and one that I continued to maintain as an investment property after taking a job in another town. A stone formed in the pit of my stomach and I felt myself begin to sweat, trying to hold down my rising panic. The tenants had been struggling to pay rent and our relationship was a bit strained. I knew they were out of town at their daughter's wedding, but what on earth could have been the cause? Little tentacles of fear threatened to creep in and take over my mind and my body. Guilt, stress, and the terror of financial ruin were knocking at my door. Even though no one was hurt, I felt so much fear building inside. I had just prayed for new windows the month before, but, seriously, Universe, this was a bit drastic! At that moment, I realized that I wasn't even sure if I had insurance on the property. I mean, a property management company oversaw the home owners association (HOA), but what exactly were the details of my insurance? What was my responsibility? What was theirs? I had no idea.

Furthermore, I knew I wasn't going to get any more information for a few days since it happened at the start of a weekend. As I teetered between panic and rationality, I felt the critical importance of this moment in time. I was faced with a choice. Would I have the courage to surrender and have faith that I was in the hands of Spirit? Or would I succumb to victimhood, fear, and extreme stress? Faced with these options, I decided to go with the prior. I put on my alchemist hat and rolled up my sleeves. I would make this a great opportunity to live beyond the external story, no matter what.

My daughters would be watching as usual, to see how I would respond to this new stressor. This was also my chance as a mom to show them how to handle an unexpected challenge. Even if it didn't appear that they were paying attention, I knew that even on some subconscious level, their brains would be registering my words and actions. Every move I made would be catalogued somewhere within their minds under "what to do when 'bad' things happen."

I'd like to report that it was that easy, but it wasn't. All weekend long I volleyed back and forth between thoughts of my potential demise and rise. Something that really helped me to ground and stabilize my thoughts was showing up to a kirtan that night. It was held in a magical place called the Starhouse, a wooden octagonal structure in the foothills surrounding Boulder, Colorado. This enchanting building sits on sacred land, land blessed with intention and ritual and saturated with the essence of spiritual practice. Overlooking the sparkling lights of Boulder, the candlelit windows glowed brightly in the twilight. As I began to release and let go through dancing and singing, a thunderstorm rolled through. I walked outside to get some air and the sky erupted in light flashes! At one point it seemed as if the universe hit the pause button on a flash and the entire sky glowed a brilliant bright blue. I stood beneath nature's show. I could feel my transcendent observer step into place to take a look at my present story, and a presence of surrender enveloped me. I felt keenly aware again that I was not in charge, that the flow of life was flowing and I had the power to simply flow with it, or not. Like the powerful flashes in the clouds, I was not in charge of the ultimate orchestration of things. Little thoughts of fear, like *How will I cover total devastation?* and *Do I have enough insurance?* began to trickle in, and I imagined a glowing bubble of light all around me, pushing the fear further away. While I couldn't dictate the flow of life, I could take charge of my response to it.

The first thing I did was to repeat to myself over and over again that I did not need to know everything. I didn't know that it was a tragedy; I didn't know that it was a loss; I didn't know if it was bad or good, all I knew was that I really, really, REALLY didn't like what was happening. Now, more than ever, was my time to be strong and to bring my best self to the situation. That Monday morning, I decided to spend this time in the unknown, getting as prepared as possible. Nothing like a total burn to get me fired into action!

I began to ask all the experts I knew for referrals: contractors, lawyers, my real estate agent, etc. I gathered other information, such as HOA insurance coverage, by-laws, names and numbers of the property management company, and insurance agents. I called my original mortgage broker to inquire about the insurance that was presented at the time I bought the property. I called my firefighter friends. At each contact, I specifically stated that I did not want sympathy, but rather wanted to empower myself with information. I was not going to allow any victim consciousness to take hold.

And finally, I called my ex-husband. I hadn't talked to him on the phone more than twice for a couple of years. But since he was a real estate/landlord guru, I felt that this might be the perfect time to put my heart vow into action. I'd vowed to find and feel my heart, to clear all that was in the way of my connection to it, to awaken my heart energies and to make peace with love. What better time than now to capitalize on this bump in the road to contact my ex-husband and see if I could deposit some peace into our terribly bankrupt energy account?

And it turned out . . . he was really helpful. I was reminded that he is a total rock star in his area of expertise. He immediately sent me HOA information, contractor information, the city building permit info, and a new management company for my continued rental situation. Hanging up the phone, I cried tears of gratitude for that small energetic deposit.

Later, I was talking on the phone to my father after picking up my daughter from camp, and I shared how supportive my ex-husband had been. Every little bit of positive energetic deposit has the power to ever-so-slightly shift any situation. This was a powerful moment in which old negative energy was being alchemized into beautiful new potential.

A few days later the investigator called me back to report that an old bathroom fan that had been left on for quite some time was the spark that eventually ignited to cause the fire. He went on to say that there was nothing anyone could have done to prevent it and that it was a common occurrence (note to everyone to change out old bathroom fans!). The insurance provided through the HOA and my own personal insurance covered an entire remodeling from the basement to the rafters and, after a long year and a half, I was the delighted owner of a brand new condo (which exponentially increased its value and income potential). While it was an unbelievably prosperous ending, it was more about the journey than anything. What I learned and practiced was priceless.

At the end of it, I felt good about having stayed focused on the positive during a majority of it all. It was as if I'd passed through what Dr. Alberto Villoldo calls in his book, *Illumination,* "an initiation, a sacred moment in life in which, if accepted, allows for death of the former self and ultimate healing." The Inca shamans believed that each of these initiations would bring a person closer to illumination. Illumination was seen as a series of awakenings and realizations that we pass through again and again, bringing about our deep healing. This was an initiation for me. My deepest prayer was for the freedom to live in my own Shangri-Love, feeling and sharing love, even when the world was burning down around me. What my soul desired was to live beyond the circumstances, knowing my essence was love regardless of the outer world.

I share this story for a couple of reasons. First, it fully illustrates what I was beginning to feel as I faced relating to and within myself instead of with a romantic other. As I stopped dating, I felt as if all that I had previously known was suddenly "burning" to the ground and, as with the event of my burning condo, I needed to integrate the intense emotions within myself. And second, I believe that fire can represent a powerful purification process. When we face our pent-up feelings, which I was being called to do in the cessation of dating, there's a chance to free them once and for all. Eckhart Tolle states in *A New Earth*, "Suffering has a noble purpose: the evolution of consciousness and the burning up of the ego." But this is only accomplished when we approach the suffering with a light of acceptance and with an activated observer. It's in staying with the burn, staying with the uncomfortable and sometimes excruciatingly painful feelings that have been stuffed down, that they are transmuted and set free. This was my next phase of development. Staying with those yuck feelings that were percolating to the surface to draw them into awareness for release. My heart often felt like it was on fire in those days of being just with me. To feel the burn, I realized that I was going to need some tools.

AGNI AND THE SPIRIT OF PURIFICATION

As I concentrated on feeling my feelings as they were coming up, I gradually made progress. Standing in the fire to feel, it was as if I had the spiritual circuitry to start over in life with a brand new me that was more available and more present to feel love and express love for myself and others. The Rigveda deity of fire was *Agni*, which is Sanskrit for "fire." This god of fire was the purifier of all things he touched. I began to think of fire in that way. Also, this seemed like a perfect start to the awakening of more awareness in my heart. In Tibetan, as noted in the book, *The Bliss of Inner Fire*, by Thubten Yeshe, inner fire is known as *lam kyi mang-*

do, meaning "the foundation stone on the path." The more I stayed with my emotions, the more this inner fire was transforming them.

In their book *The Seven Spiritual Laws of Yoga,* Deepak Chopra, MD, and David Simon, MD, explain, "The word *agni* is the root of the English word ignite. When your agni is burning brightly, you are capable of digesting the energy and information you ingest on a daily basis, be it food, ideas, or emotional experiences." This I found to be true. As I felt the pain of my repressed emotions, I eventually felt purified. Riding the waves of emotional pain without running away, I was freeing the grips the pain had on me.

I found comfort in *The Radiance Sutras* by Lorin Roche, PhD. This book was filled with meditations to ignite my soul's inner fire. As he suggested in the book, for a few days I lived immersed in the meditation that read, "I am immersed in the flame, the flame of Life. The universal fire flows through me without resistance." I allowed the fire of emotion to burn wild and free within, setting my dormant heart free in order to feel more joy. My experience was not unlike how gold is purified and transformed by plunging it into the fire, not just the outer edges of fire, but into the heart of the fire where it is the hottest blue. Just as gold is transformed and formed within the hottest flame, so are we. By staying with the burn, I would find my own phoenix of love rising from the ashes of what had been my lifelong search for love. And, little did I know that this bird was waiting for me just around the corner.

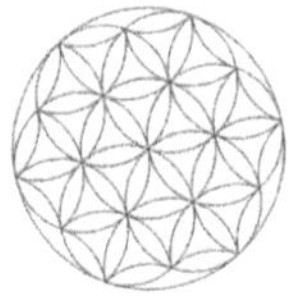

Shangri-Love Activities:
To Purify Your Heart Energy and Activate Your Inner Fire, Your Agni

SUN SALUTATIONS

There are many ways to activate your inner fire, or agni, and to stimulate the release of strong emotions. I love the sun salutations included in Deepak Chopra and David Simon's book, *The Seven Spiritual Laws of Yoga*. In the book, they outline the twelve poses of the sun salutations, which, according to the authors, "are designed to awaken the connection between your *agni*, or inner fire, and that of the sun." They expand on this, saying, "When practiced along with following a healthy diet, a good daily routine, and the conscious avoidance of physical and emotional toxicity, the sun salutations are designed to kindle your inner fire so you can radiate the best of who you are."

BREATH OF FIRE

One of my all-time favorite practices is something called the "Breath of Fire," which is taught in Kundalini Yoga practice. This breath invariably supports me in stimulating my body and emotional release. It is recommended that you start with a slow rhythm and only practice three minutes initially, working your way up to longer practice. Stop if it doesn't feel good or causes you increased distress in the body such as lightheadedness. Also, this exercise is not for those who struggle with heart disease or high blood pressure. Please do further research and/or consult your health practitioner before engaging in breathwork. Kundalini teachers suggest that breath of fire has a multitude of health benefits, including blood purification, stimulation and balance of the nervous system, and synchronization of the entire body.

Instructions: Inhale and exhale through the nose. Each inhalation and exhalation should be of equal length. As you breathe in, expand your belly outward. As you breathe out, contract your belly inward. Your belly should be moving in and out much like a pump. There are many videos online that have more comprehensive breath of fire instruction. Gabrielle Bernstein has some wonderful breath of fire meditations that can be found through a search on YouTube or an online search engine.

DANCE WITH YOUR INNER FIRE

Move, swirl, jump, pounce, stomp, leap, twirl, pulse, and dance with your inner fire. Put on music that stimulates your inner passion and ignites your soul. Dance out those stuck emotions. Meet them right where they are and release and accept them, allowing them to flow through dance and movement. Seduce them into the light of your awareness and let them be, letting them go and flow through your body as you move.

CHAPTER 4:

BECOMING A PHOENIX OF LOVE

Holding back feelings is the beginning of separation. Sharing them is the ending of it.
~Paul Ferrini

As I was standing in the fire of my emotions to reconnect within myself and to develop a relationship within, I began to be able to really sense what was going on inside. Something deep within my heart started to open just a little and it felt good. It felt like love was rising from the ashes of my past; a phoenix of love was spreading its wings to take flight in my life. This was my process, my path, but one that I believe can melt the chains that hold any heart, including your own.

CALMING THE MEAN GIRL INSIDE

The most important thing that occurred during this time of getting to know myself was that as my life got more silent on the outside, I was able to more clearly hear what was going on *inside* of me. And, know what? I wasn't initially impressed with what I found. There was this "mean girl" talking to me in my mind and she wasn't nice. She would say things like, *What is your problem?* or *What in the world did you do that for?* or the most lethal, *You can NOT feel that way!* She was also especially loud when I fell down and engaged with my inner child in an argument, either at work or with my ex-husband or with my daughters. With all her chatter, I could finally understand why I had been running so long—it was to get away from her incessant negative jabs! I wondered how I could ever expect others to respect me in relationship, when my own internal voice was not respectful.

So I began to develop my own "soul mantras." A mantra is a word or a phrase that is repeated over and over again to infuse a certain meaning into the mind and body. I called them soul mantras because I felt like when I said them, I was sending messages directly to my soul. I began to talk to myself like I'd wanted my Prince Charming to talk to me. When I "fell down" or made a mistake, I would say things like *That's okay, you are just learning, love. Let's try again.* When I felt sad, I would soothe myself by saying, *I love you, I know you are doing the best you can.* When I fell down at work, I would call my work number and leave a voicemail for myself on the morning commute so I could listen and replay it throughout the day. I would say, *You're doing a good job, keep it up!* I even sent myself an email love letter once. I thought, well, if I wasn't seeking attention from men, then I would become the best lover I ever had. I would speak to me in the best love song! And, you know, it wasn't about lying to myself. Of course there were times when I really didn't like something I'd done. In those moments, I knew it was the most critical time to be there for me, so I would tell myself, *I really don't like that decision you made or that behavior, but I know you can make a different choice now and can put some positive energy back into the system. Let's see what we can do to get back to feeling good.* I was quickly getting the hang of it. It was like I was creating a home for the spirit within me.

Sonia Choquette enlightened me to this concept in her book, *The Answer is Simple*, in which she discusses giving our spirits a "healthy, happy home to dwell in." She explains that neglect is one reason that our spirits don't feel at home. Other causes include toxic substances, lack of contact with nature, and sedentary, stagnant living. Our spirits also vacate the premises in the face of extreme fear or trauma. This concept resonated with me. As I was quickly becoming my own good friend, one I could rely on especially when things got tough, I was creating a home for my spirit. And in this inner sanctuary, I could take refuge within the stillness of my own soul when the outside world felt harsh or uncertain. I can hardly put into words just how much relief this brought me.

ASHES OF ME

As I was empowering myself with kind words and creating a soft place to land within my mind and heart, I got in touch with the actual pain that I used to feel as a result of trying to coerce love outside myself. I came across an old journal entry that was a perfect example of the pain I'd experienced in the midst of my relationship dramas: *I'm here again on my knees, again in desperation. I've lit the candles. The altar is glowing, decorated with crystals and images of love and spiritual treasures.* [Note: I was pleading with God, even though I knew better, even though I knew that pleading prayer was really just creating more of what I didn't want.] *Please, I prayed, release my fears, resentments, sensitivity to judgment, anger, feelings of being controlled and at the mercy of others, abandonment . . . Please heal all of this. Strike it from me, Dear Spirit, release me! And . . . then help me to form positive, strong, healthy, intimate, relationships. Make me feel loveable! Take away my loneliness, this deep loneliness that I feel even when I am with people. Take it away, dear God, dear angels. Take it away! Please help me to be strong for my girls! Heal this sad victimhood! I want to feel held and comforted. Dear Holy Spirit, I give this darkness to you. Open my heart so completely that all of this darkness is banished.*

This is a perfect example of countless journal entries written during my dating escapades. I've always been a journaler, getting in touch with my feelings through the power of words. I began journaling at the age of nine and never stopped. My first journal was a tiny, yellow book that had a lock and key. Each page had five entry spaces for each day. Even at the age of nine, that was never enough space for all that I wanted to say. I can remember as a small child looking out across the farmlands from my bedroom window and hearing my thoughts in a sort of narration in my head, kind of like a movie. When I wrote my thoughts down, somehow I felt more "real," as if, until I communicated through writing, I wasn't quite able to process everything that happened in my life.

So, given the small blanks on the page, I began to use extra little squares of paper (shaped like a sticky note but without the "sticky"), and wrote more of my story for each page, folding and sticking them in the page of the week that corresponded. Fairly soon the journal's little clasp would hardly close because there were so many little papers inside!

This particular journal entry was written at the demise of yet another of my relationships; one that I'd felt had great potential. Reading the words that were angrily scribed within a journal since bent and twisted from water damage, I could feel sadness dripping from the pages. Compassion bubbled up within me as I read my thoughts about feeling completely alone, like I was the last being on the planet and like there was an impenetrable barrier around me that no one could get through. I'd felt like a big giant failure and shame seeped from my pen as I considered that I'd created yet another instance of modeling misguided relationship for my daughters. This pain was the "ashes of me," the remnants from years of trying to pin down love that was always moving just out of my reach.

Reading these words motivated me to reach deeper, to seek further within me for the answers. I felt like I was slowly unlocking my heart and getting more closely in touch with how I felt inside. These journal entries helped me to feel some of the pulse points of my pain, providing a closer look at the patterns in my life that were masking my underlying feelings of sadness, frustration, anger, and fear. I was beginning to feel differently now, more at peace, but there were still moments when these old feelings would surface.

Getting Authentic

So I had the mean girl calmed down, I was creating a home for my spirit, but still I found myself a bit wiggly in the attempt to really feel and know what was going on inside me. I was trying to look myself directly in the mirror and to *not* wiggle as I contemplated what was going on inside. It reminded me of Carlos Castaneda's book *The Active Side of Infinity* where he is apprenticing with Juan Matus, a Yaqui Indian shaman from Mexico. Carlos goes to visit his master teacher, Juan, and shares his reverence for a professor of cognition with whom he is studying at the university. Juan warns Carlos not to make others into "mythological creatures" through great admiration, and encourages him to get closer to the professor. After months of trying to connect, Carlos finds the professor elusive and evasive. Finally, Juan expresses his

> "abhorrence of timid souls who shy away from interaction to the point where even though they interact, they merely infer or deduce, in terms of their own psychological states, what is going on without actually perceiving what is really going on. They interact without ever being part of the interaction."

In the formation of my inner sanctuary, I felt a bit like I was the "timid soul," shying away from interaction with my inner self, sometimes neglecting the deeper feelings and only paying attention to my surface story. In this way, I was sort of like Carlos seeking his professor who was the timid soul that shied away from authentic interaction; the only difference was that it was me seeking myself.

In my attempts to connect within, I had to be present to many of the ways I had, mostly unconsciously, wiggled away from my own deeper knowing of myself, my feelings, my thoughts, and my innermost wishes and desires. Most of all, I had wiggled away from touching that part of me that is the experience of love; my soul. And, until this point, I had been shying away from this connection by seeking love outside myself. This process is a task of infinite proportion since my soul is in the process of continuous refinement and expansion, but it was time to actually get started in earnest. No more wiggling! I was going to finally find love, touch love, and experience love within myself, rather than running around like a chicken chasing rainbows outside me. But, I had a couple of other stops to make, to really clear out the old pain, memories, grievances, and behaviors. The first thing that really, *really* helped me was forgiveness.

HO'OPONOPONO: THE FORGIVENESS FAIRY

While I'd made some progress in my efforts to calm down my inner mean girl and get in touch with my feelings, I was still hitting bumps in the road where grievances would pop up and I would find myself on a mental detour into finding fault, judging what should be different, and holding on to past stuff. I needed a spiritual vacuum cleaner, something to help me clear out and release the old.

There's a Hawaiian shamanic ritual called ho'oponopono that provides a way of cleansing negative memories, unconscious fears, and dysfunctional programming to grant oneself forgiveness, peace, and love. For me, it was a way to take full responsibility for my life and draw my power back to myself.

The Book of Ho'oponopono, written by Luc Bodin, MD, Nathalie Bodin Lamboy, and Jean Graciet, likens the practice of taking 100 percent responsibility for one's life to viewing images from a slide projector on a screen. They suggest imagining that there's a slide that produces an intense reaction within you. In response, you take a knife and rip the screen, only to see that the slide continues to project on the wall behind. So, you get a jackhammer to break down the wall. Still there is that offending image continuing to project. What ho'oponopono does is to help us to change the slide, thus changing the perception of our mental projection!

A phrase from the book's foreword explains it perfectly:
"Cleansing takes place in three stages. First
we must open our hearts; then, we welcome
'what is' with love. Finally, we have to learn
to let go of the veil, stop clinging, and trust
in the God we all carry within ourselves."

I had opened my heart with my sankalpa, and now I was in the process of welcoming "what is" with love. I wanted a more profound ability to feel and share love within myself and with others; to get to that place, I sensed that it was necessary to transmute the fear in my heart into love.

Ho'oponopono connects accepting "what is" and self-responsibility to self- forgiveness. The forgiveness mantra goes like this:

I'm sorry. Please forgive me. Thank you, I love you.

It was such a powerful process to repeat this mantra over and over again. I was repeating these words from myself to myself, letting go of past grievances while simultaneously sending the message to my subconscious that I always had the power to choose my response in life. I was also using these words when I came across new situations or events that I found fault with. As I continued to recite the mantra and work with it over time, I began to understand at a deeper level that I am responsible for everything in my life, responsible for *all* of my experiences. See, when I accepted responsibility, I took my power back. I now had the power to shift my experience from feelings of victim to feelings of empowerment. Every time I encountered an experience, thought, or memory that squeezed my heart and I felt myself begin to close down, I recited this mantra to myself. The more I recited, the more I let go of the negativity, the lighter and freer I felt. Instead of victimhood onto the screen of my life, I was now beginning to project taking full responsibility.

Ho'oponopono helped me shift negativity in a big way. The more I used it, the more I felt like a forgiveness fairy was flitting around me, touching on painful memories and beliefs and setting them free. I also began to see that every moment is a choice to open my heart more in love or to contract my heart in fear. The more I let go of old energy, the lighter and freer my heart felt. It wasn't overnight, but rather a gradual shift over time.

Writing a New Story Within

According to the Law of Attraction, we draw to us what we put our focus on. I kept writing affirmations, taping them to the mirror, reciting them in my car, singing them, and attempting to infuse them with feeling, but sometimes it felt a bit silly and like nothing was happening. I kept being mindful of how I was talking to myself and was using my soul mantras. And, while I was feeling better, I still was missing something.

Even though it looked like I was asking God for a change, I was still beseeching a God that was outside me. It was like I believed if I sang louder, the message might just get through. There was a part of me that needed to address my belief systems at a deeper level. Consciously, I was hitting the target with my soul mantras and this was a good start, but if I was going to really get some sustainable change, I needed to get to the roots, the core belief systems that were operating. That's when I found Neurosculpting®.

Lisa Wimberger, founder of the Neurosculpting Institute, defines Neurosculpting in her book, *Neurosculpting: A Whole-Brain Approach to Heal Trauma, Rewrite Limiting Beliefs and Find Wholeness*, as "a mental training process that quiets our fight-or-flight center and activates our prefrontal cortex, which is the mind's seat of our compassion and empathy." This mental training process, while occupying and engaging my linear left brain, activated my right brain simultaneously so that I could begin to write and create new stories and beliefs within me. It was the perfect tool to support my intentional creation of new ways of thinking and new belief systems. The more I neurosculpted new stories within my brain, calmed down my overactive fight-or-flight system, and activated the more compassionate part of my brain, the prefrontal cortex, the more I had options as to how I would respond in life. I was no longer at the mercy of my feelings, but was becoming more able to decide how I would respond to life's more difficult moments.

As I was undergoing this process of completely revamping my internal mental processes and cleansing away old energy and memories, I took to heart the ho'oponopono authors' suggestion that it was necessary to give the mind something to do so that it would more graciously "let go" during the process.

Generally speaking, the mind doesn't want to let go. To let go is to lose control and the mind likes nothing better than to play game of "I think I know everything: how things *should* be, how they *should* go, how I or others *should* feel" (the key word in all of this is *should*). I attended the Warrior One and Two Neurosculpting classes where Lisa guided us in learning how to manage our internal thought and energy systems and taught us specific techniques for calming down our nervous systems, (mine had been in "overdrive" all these years and was causing inflammation and tension in my muscles and joints). Lisa's meditation approach was so powerful that I became trained as a coach so I could share it with others, including the kids I worked with in the schools.

Heart Wings

Gradually, through the ho'oponopono mantra, Neurosculpting, and development of my inner sanctuary, I gained more and more access to my heart (a process that continues today) and began to feel lighter and freer. It was as if I was flourishing a garden inside myself. I began to live my life more from the inside than the outside, which changed the course of my life from within. It was like Don Miguel Ruiz so eloquently captures in his book, *The Toltec Art of Life and Death*: "Ounce by ounce, he made his heart a weightless thing, emptying it of a thousand lies." I felt like I was gaining on the emptying out of my heart so that it was freer for more living, more expression, more love. The soul mantras, meditation, and forgiveness practice were starting to clear away the intense emotions that I'd been carrying for so long. The lightness that resulted felt like wings, and I've come to refer to these "wings" as "heart wings." During this period, I thought back to the first time I got in touch with my heart wings many years before, when I was just starting out as a school psychologist.

I'd been assigned an internship at one of the toughest high schools in the inner city of Denver. I referred to it as "the front lines of education" because on some days it felt like I was going to battle with many an unseen enemy. These students faced many obstacles to their education. There were low socioeconomic statuses, drugs, teen pregnancies, homelessness, dropouts, and chaotic homes of various dysfunction. Some days I was a bit terrified going to work. Picture this, a petite, Pollyanna-ish, blonde girl attempting to provide psychological services in the barrio. Although I spoke fluent Spanish, which was one reason I was placed there, I wasn't exactly what you would call a "natural fit." There were often bloody fights in the hallways. One day found discarded drug paraphernalia in the corner of the locker area. Each morning I would step over lounging students making out on the floor as I made my way to a tiny closet office with no window, in a basement corner of the school. I tried to maintain my composure one day as I interviewed a student wearing yellow "cat eye" contact lenses. I remember not knowing how to make eye contact or where to look as I attempted to focus on my interview to gather information for a special education meeting. Another student, seemingly high on a substance, asked in a counseling session if I was a drug dealer. Needless to say, I was a bit out of my league until I learned some tools.

As I continued to show up that year, I learned a lot from the hearts of these struggling students. They taught me to look way beyond all appearances to feel deeply into the heart of the situations to determine the ultimate need of all at the table. They taught me the value of listening and truly hearing what is being communicated beyond words. They taught me gumption, perseverance, and the value of staying the course, even when it seems like there is no positive outcome. They taught me resilience in its highest form, the kind of resilience born of survival skills that had polished their ability to face the extreme difficulties in life.

The year progressed and I began to play a little in my imagination on the way to work. While commuting, sometimes dreading another long day of trying to locate students who were rarely at school, I began to pray. I visualized battalions of angels surrounding the school. Then I visualized myself with wings. I found increasing comfort and peace imagining my wings. In my imagination, I would become like an angel with glorious wings outstretched behind me as I walked through the dark halls.

Lo and behold, the more I imagined my wings, the more I seemed to become visible to the students. I was finally able to develop a relationship with several students and started teaching Jon Kabat-Zinn's mindfulness tools and concepts from his book *Wherever You Go, There You Are* in a math class. I still laugh when I think about the first day I proudly faced the class and announced the title of the book. A gruff-looking boy slouching in the back row responded, "Well,

duh, Miss, wherever I go, there I am." It was the perfect start to a deeper conversation.

Those days in the inner city high school were my first glimpses of heart wings. Now, I felt my heart wings were growing again, yet this time with greater impact. I've always been fascinated by the idea that if humans had wings, they would be attached at the backside of the heart. In reactivating these heart wings, I was beginning to select the raw materials for a new way of being, and I was loving the new universe that was being created. In this way, I was becoming the artist of my life, engaging my soul now in the creative process!

My wings were growing, just like the wings of a phoenix of love rising from the ashes of all that no longer served my life. They were my heart wings. But it would require further refinement for them to actually take flight. In order to live more from love and less from fear, there was much more I needed to know, to explore, and to integrate. I'm sure many parents can identify with the concept that our children are our greatest teachers. Wouldn't you know, just around the corner, one of my teachers was gearing up to show me more about the nature of wings and flight.

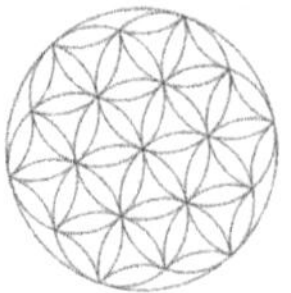

Shangri-Love Activities:
SOUL MANTRAS

Find a quiet place where you can sit. Calm your mind for a while by breathing in the stillness. Draw into your imagination the caring words you would love to hear from a dear friend or a loved one. Imagine what sorts of phrases you would say to your dear friend if she called in distress. How would you comfort her? What would you say? Now take out a journal and record all these phrases. Create notes to carry with you throughout the day to look at, recite, and practice whenever you are feeling down or frustrated. Self-soothing is an art and is individually unique to each one of us. You have your own love language. Listen to your heart and whisper those words of love to yourself often, in a loving, compassionate voice. Send yourself a love message on your voicemail at work, email some love to your inbox, and set reminders with soul mantras on your phone.

HO'OPONOPONO

My prayer partner and I sometimes recite ho'oponopono out loud for several minutes at the beginning of our prayer time. This mantra carries a beautiful energy that neutralizes any hurt, resentment, or other negative emotion, opening the heart for love to shine out and through. Sometimes we hold the world in our prayers as we recite. Other times we hold a specific event, feeling, or instance that is calling out for a positive shift. I encourage you to recite this mantra at the onset of any grievance or negative energy. I like to recite it while holding my mala beads. I hold the 108 beads and recite a ho'oponopono mantra for each bead, moving to the next bead after each recitation until I reach the end.

CHAPTER 5:

HEART WINGS

Wings have long been associated with the heart. In the Sufi tradition, the mystical branch of Islam, the symbol of their order is a winged heart with a crescent in the center. They believe that the heart is between the soul and the body, a sort of divine messenger between spirit and matter. Symbol-dictionary.net explains "the crescent in the heart of the Sufi wings represents that the heart, responsive to the light of God, is illuminated." In ancient Egypt, wings were a symbol of spiritual progress, a symbol of the heart reaching upward toward heaven.

So what are these so-called heart wings I'm talking about? Wings embody the inherent lightness of being that comes about when you release whatever energy is protecting/defending your psyche, allowing your deepest heart to shine. When your heart wings unfold, you are more in touch with your intuition and more apt to feel open and joyful. When you are "minding" your wings—which means to recognize, listen deeply to, and acknowledge them—then you naturally radiate love from within yourself, effortlessly and vibrantly. You are, in your deepest essence, an expression of love. It isn't something that you "DO" or "think about," but rather, it's simply a way of being.

I let on in the last chapter that one of my greatest teachers was just around the corner ready to show me more about living from the heart. Well, this teacher was my daughter, Maddie (my daughters Maiya and Maddie have been two of my greatest teachers in life). Maddie was the one who invited me to "mind the wings."

TAILS AND WINGS

As I was spending more time practicing forgiveness and letting go, using my soul mantras to build my capacity for self-compassion and calming down my nervous system with Neurosculpting, I began to feel lighter. And as I explored the newfound lightness dawning in my own heart, my daughter Maddie, through her art, reminded me how simple it is to begin heart-centered living.

From birth, Maddie came into the world with great big expression. She was a born artist. In diapers, she would spend hours drawing tiny perfect circles on paper. She creates art in every form and modality, rom pencil and paper, to paint, to clay, to interior designs of rooms. She has an enormous imagination. Once, she fashioned a mermaid tail from flip-flops, duct tape, and garden mats and asked me to take her to the athletic club to test the tail's "glide efficiency."

Next came the construction of wings. Armed with a self-drawn and designed pattern, she spent days fashioning her creation. There were feathers in every corner of the house, some even hot glued to the carpet. She soon announced that she'd achieved success. She told me not to look as she led me upstairs to her room. Opening the door, I was speechless. There was the most beautiful pair of wings that I could ever imagine. Each feather was mindfully placed with love.

"What are you going to do with the wings?" I asked. "Wear them to school for Halloween!" she answered, looking at me with the "seriously, Mom" expression. As a mom *and* a school psychologist, I kept asking more questions, such as "How will you sit at your desk?" "Will the teachers care?" "Won't the other students bump into you in the hallway?" But each time, she patiently assured me that it was more than possible, in fact, she said, the other students would just have to "mind the wings."

The morning of her angelic flight arrived. She bubbled with excitement as we gingerly placed the wings in the back seat of the car. I pulled up in front of the school. She quickly tied them onto her back. I kissed her cheek as she joyfully marched away. Wiping tears, I snapped some quick pictures as she flew, merging with the throng of students heading toward the school doors. With a last, giant smile she looked back at me and floated out of view into the crowd.

This Halloween happened a year into my Shangri-Love journey. Here, right in front of me, was a wonderful model of a heart fully open. I felt the impact of her example. I compared her lack of self-consciousness to the wings on my own heart. I realized in watching her flight through the middle school doors that the energetic wings of my heart were still quite furled up securely in the middle of my back. She listened to her heart, and regardless of the greater opinion of the outside world or any naysayers, simply created what she found there. I, on the other hand, still felt some heaviness inside. I still felt fairly scattered from judgments and some victimhood thoughts regarding the events of my life thus far. After years of self-protected shallow relationships, I felt scared to express my true feelings and to share them with others. I was lacking a sense of inner trust and couldn't quite discern from time to time what was truly "for me" and what I was simply doing in order to gain approval from others. All of this kept my wings more tightly furled. Maddie, on the other hand, was living full out from the impulse of love within her, unabashedly sharing it with the world. I wanted to expand my wings that way too!

With Maddie's flight, I felt something in my soul begin to stir. She had said to "mind the wings." What would happen in my life if I began to mind my own heart wings by paying more attention to the inner impulses and nudges from my heart? How could I release even more energy around victim thoughts and feel more centered? Could I begin to allow love to step even more ahead of fear to guide more of my steps in life?

What I found, the more I asked these questions and meditated on the answers, was that I naturally moved from being resonant with fear and strife to being resonant with love. I was guided to the steps necessary to more fully open my heart to love and to let go of the fear that had so long been keeping my wings furled. The first step in minding my wings was to activate my observer while allowing my thoughts to flow on through me.

OBSERVING THE THOUGHT TRAINS

As I continued to be present with the feelings rising up within me, I realized how many of them really had to do with feelings of powerlessness and victimhood. I was truly enjoying parenting my two daughters, but sometimes, particularly when one of them was struggling with something or I took on a lot of work, I felt overwhelmed and alone. In those moments I would start to fixate on my thoughts and spiral into heavy feelings. I wanted to make a complete shift from my thoughts, however subtle, of *I need you to change for me to feel good,* or *I need my bank account, the government, my children's behavior, or any other external circumstance to shift for me to feel peace.* I wanted to feel peace simply because I connected to the peace inside me. This was, I felt, an attribute of living from my heart.

How would I make these shifts? While Neurosculpting and ho'oponopono were tremendous supports, I also felt like a shift in perspective, actively shifting my focal point from looking outside to looking inside, would help me as well.

Remember the transcendent observer from before? Well, now I was going to activate that observer and add another layer. I would step back from my different stories, identifying with them less and less, and focus on allowing my thoughts to be and observing them with curiosity, rather than using my will and mind power to change them. This was a huge shift in my mindset and one that required, and still requires, lots of practice.

An example of how my thoughts would typically run was one time when I was flipping through *Travel and Leisure* to "armchair travel," something I like to do often. I read a feature article about a beautiful bungalow sitting right on the ocean in Bali. I imagined lounging by the infinity pool with a book and sparkly fruit juice elixir. Immediately, however, my thoughts began to swirl and stir up all sorts of things, one thought leading to another. From the thought of *What a beautiful bungalow, I would love to visit,* I would think, *Oh, it's $500 per night.* And *I should be a better entrepreneur and supplement my income more,* and *How am I going to pay for the removal of the humongous cottonwood that is threatening the roof of the house?* and *My daughter wants voice lessons.* That cascade began with seeing a beautiful bungalow in Bali! There went the train of thought into Worryville.

I started to practice catching the cascade at its onset. What if I began to simply allow my Bali bungalow thought to just *be*? *What a beautiful bungalow in Bali, I would like to visit.* With my transcendent observer activated, I would allow that thought to appear and to simply flow on by. That way my heart, instead of contracting in fear, would stay open to what was present. And, if the train to Worryville left the station and I started to feel anxious, then I would simply observe *that* and let it be. It was all about a new way of being with what was going on within me.

This stage of allowing was a deeper letting go than I had ever experienced. Before, I typically felt that my negative thoughts were "bad" and tried to stop them from happening. Now, I was noticing their existence and opening a space of acknowledgment without attachment to changing them, just allowing them to float on by and through me, unobstructed by any sort of manipulation or getting stuck on my mind's dam of trying to figure everything out.

ONE HUNDRED PERCENT RESPONSIBILITY

The second part of this process of letting go was in taking full responsibility for my feelings and my life. This was a 180-degree turn. My wings were unfurled, folded up because of many thoughts of powerlessness, such as *I am all alone in parenting and don't have a partner to problem-solve the girl's ups and downs with.* When I would think a thought such as this, I worked on observing it—along with the associated feeling—and allowing it to be. Then I would decide what action I wanted to take to shift within myself.

Assuming this level of responsibility brought my energy completely back to me and within that sphere, there was the power to create my own reality and to truly follow my heart's guidance without apology. Creating my own reality meant that I would decide how I would respond to life. In stepping back, I now had the space to do that.

I had grown up thinking that everyone and everything outside me dictated how I felt. My focus was entirely externally based. If you liked me, then I was okay. If you didn't like me, I was not okay. In this way I did not take responsibility for myself nor did I learn how to.

When I first started awakening and trying out these concepts, I was working with New York transformational life coach, Seran Wilkie. She was the ultimate at delivering it to me straight up when my thinking wasn't aligned with taking responsibility for me. She showed me again and again where I was giving away my power to others in thinking that somehow they were in charge of me. My biggest clues were the thoughts . . . *They should change . . .* [fill in the blank] or *I know how things should be . . . I know that this is wrong . . . I know this is right . . . I am somehow superior . . . I am somehow inferior . . . I am somehow justified because . . . .* These thoughts firmly placed my power outside me. If the other person could change something and make me feel better as a result, then I was linking the other person to my feelings. From now on I would shift my dependence on others to dictate how I felt.

I see this taught all the time in the schools. Teachers say to students, "Who are you in charge of?" to which they are supposed to respond, "me." Yet soon afterwards they will announce to the class, "You are making me mad. You are disappointing me." This is an example of where the confusion begins. I know I've done this too as a parent. It is a subtle process, but one that gets powerfully entrenched in the mind. Before, the student was told that he was only in charge of himself, and then the teacher tells him that he is essentially in charge of the way the teacher feels.

What I did know was that I was beginning to feel freer. My heart felt free of the weight of all those years of being erroneously in charge of all sorts of things outside myself, things I had no control over but was trying to take charge of. By pulling my focus back to me and taking responsibility for my feelings, I was suddenly able to help myself to feel better. And what was my biggest clue if my heart was opening or contracting? How I was feeling. Any time I began to sense a shift in my energy toward the negative, I would pause, activate my observer, and witness my thoughts. Soon, I began to see links between my thoughts. I began to identify thoughts where I was judging others or myself, thoughts where I was blaming others and not taking responsibility for my feelings, and then I was able to let them go.

Here's a word of caution though, about this process. I believe the extent of our ability to take 100 percent responsibility for our lives is directly proportional to the amount of self-acceptance and compassion we have for ourselves. The more we have built the capacity of self-compassion and unconditional acceptance within ourselves, the more ability we have to assume full responsibility for our actions and our life as a whole.

If that inner mean girl is still talking and judging, then the tendency to project onto the external environment can be nearly overwhelming because the pain is intense. When I began this process of 100 percent responsibility, I began to realize the ways that victim consciousness was ruling my life, resulting in my blame and egoic views of others. My first tendency was to use this awareness as an excuse to feel even more terrible, to tear myself down even more. I would hang up the phone with my coach and feel like a slug, a leach, a slimy slithering thing. And on other days, I would be seething with anger *at her* for pointing out those places in me that still wanted to play the victim.

There's a natural tendency within us to run away or deny our feelings when we hurt. When this happens, activate that observer and separate from the story again and again to support your evolution during this process. It is through practice and repetition that we build new ways of being in the world. Return again and again with love—that is what it means to mind your heart wings. Be gentle with yourself and over time, with greater mindfulness of your heart wings, they will slowly unfurl.

RESONANCE

The more time I spent minding my heart wings, the more I began to discern what was "for me" in any given instant. I could differentiate what resonated with my heart and what did not. And the freer I felt, the easier it was to discern.

I was first introduced to the concept of resonance at an early age in my dad's ham radio shack. My father is an engineer and an amateur radio operator; since he was a little boy, he built radios. This "ham shack," to which it was affectionately referred by my family, was my dad's office. It was an enchanting place. The walls were paneled with wood from an old barn that had blown down on our farm. There were brilliantly colored postcards from as far as Russia detailing the "call names" of other amateur radio operators with whom my father had communicated. Small drawers with transistors and LED lights sat on his workbench, which also housed his various radios, a Morse code machine, and other wondrous gadgets. An old 1920s teletype machine, a precursor of the fax machine, sat in the corner. If you wanted a place to feed the imagination, this was it. I could sit in there and watch him send Morse code to people all over the world. This small-town farm girl suddenly had an entire world at her fingertips—Russia and China were alive in the room!

In conversations with my dad about resonance, frequency, and crystal radios, I considered the nature of frequency and resonance and how it might relate to other vibrations of life. Dad explained to me what frequency and resonance are like. A frequency is the vibration or oscillation around a neutral point expressed in hertz (Hz), which is really cycles, or electromagnetic energy oscillations per second. By virtue of the physical electrical characteristics of materials and an object's dimensions and geometry, it will be resonant to some frequency. Antennas and circuits are designed by constructing materials with dimensions, such that they are resonant to the "frequency of interest." Sound vibrations are in the realm of hertz and kilohertz. Radio vibrations are in a higher realm of frequencies known as kilohertz, megahertz and gigahertz. Microwave, infrared, and ultraviolet vibrations (light) go higher yet. And it goes even higher; we're just discovering uses for these frequencies.

What could this possibly have to do with the heart and heart wings? His discussion of resonance and frequencies is a metaphor for the power of our hearts. He told me that everything is resonant to something. This is a powerful concept. As I was cultivating access to my heart through minding my heart wings, I felt I was becoming resonant with higher and higher vibrations of love.

In my journey into Shangri-Love, I found that the more I connected and listened to my heart, the more it became my global positioning system (GPS) and showed me what is "for me" and what is "not for me." It reminds me of an excerpt from a poem, "Stay Close, My Heart" by Rumi (translation by Rassouli, from the *Rumi Oracle* by Alana Fairchild), where it seems to me he is encouraging us to turn within and be fully present to what resonates with our heart and nourishes our soul and what doesn't:

> *Stay close to those who know about the heart.*
> *Choose the shade of a tree*
> *That is in constant bloom.*
>
> *Don't meander aimlessly*
> *among the herb sellers and potion venders.*

Go directly to the shop
That sells nothing but sweets!

Don't sit waiting by every boiling pot
To have your plate filled!
Not every boiling pot
Is cooking what you want.

Not every sugar cane is filled with sugar.
Not every down has an up.
Not every eye has a vision.
Not every sea contains pearls.

Rumi speaks of this discernment that comes from the heart. He invites us here to be aware, to pay attention that not every invitation in life is "sweet," even though some invitations seem tasty. For instance, while I was dating in Neverland, I said yes to nearly every invitation. I wasn't listening or tuning into my heart. If I had been, I might have avoided that strange date with the Marilyn Monroe lover/personal trainer. I might have recognized the initial signs on the phone that he was "playing me" or just fooling around to see if he could get me to buy him dinner. Or I may have sensed that he was speaking sweetly but his energy was relaying a different message entirely. But in my desperation for attention, my mind-driven attempt to distract myself from my life and avoid the pain of divorce, I missed the signs.

What I was learning in minding my wings was that my heart does not lead me astray. Ever. My heart knows, my heart senses what is for my highest good. If I pay attention and tune in, I can feel the resonance of love. I can feel if something resonates more with love or more with fear. This is my heart-centered practice of minding my wings. This practice is what strengthens my ability to truly trust my heart to guide me, to illuminate my path. It is in this practice of stillness, in this practice of turning within again and again, that my heart wings truly unfold.

My Broken Wing

Ironically, just as I was just setting out to find out what it meant to mind my heart wings, I woke up one day with a "broken wing." During the night, and for a period of time leading up to this point, my shoulder had completely and excruciatingly, painfully FROZEN. I couldn't access my armpit or move my arm freely. The irony wasn't lost on me of being in the process of learning to mind my wings—even speaking in public *about* my wings—and suddenly having a broken one. Of course Spirit was attempting to support me in diving deeper within to unfold more of me and release deeper stuck energy that was contributing to my broken wing.

I visited myriad health practitioners and energy healers, even had a magnetic resonance imaging (MRI) test, where the medical diagnosis was a "bone spur." They offered surgery, but couldn't *really* guarantee that it would help at all. In fact, they acknowledged, "You will probably feel the worst you have ever felt if you do it." *That* didn't sound like my route to healing! But then one day I found a retired doctor who guided me in a meditation that completely awakened me to the intricacies and knots that had built up over the years to cause the present condition. I also was blessed to find another myofascial release "shoulder whisperer" who began to work with individual trigger points to release the muscle restrictions on the bones.

Slowly over the next few months, I began to "walk the path" backwards, untying the knots of stress that had accumulated due to stress and some injury. It was the subtlest movements that would release the muscle. Softness and gentleness were the most powerful release mechanisms. If I leaned into the exquisitely tender trigger points, they would eventually release and find peace. Slowly, with infinite patience, I regained the use of my broken wing.

This process awakened within me a deeper awareness of the world within me, not just within my heart, but within my entire being. Every muscle interconnected to the greater whole, and it was by leaning into the pain, rather than running from it or resisting it, that I regained my freedom. The same is true for the heart. It is more greatly accessed by leaning into the present moment experience rather than pushing or turning away from what is present. With my frozen shoulder, life slowed me down to go within once again, and, in doing so, I regained my wing. This slowing down was just the ticket to continue to strengthen the bridge between my heart and mind.

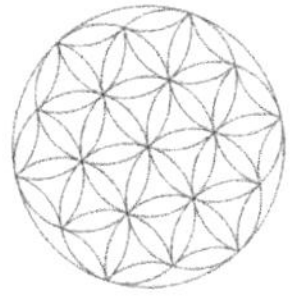

Shangri-Love Activities:
ACTIVATE YOUR TRANSCENDENT OBSERVER

Close your eyes and draw into your awareness the difference between your transcendent observer and the story of your life. There is a part of you that never changes: it's eternal; it's your essence. This observer, or wise self, is not impacted by stories, emotions, or the conditions of your life. It just IS. It is love. There is the other part of you that engages in the stories of your life. Some call this the ego or the small self. This part is engaged in and attached to drama. It identifies with conditions in order to get its bearings, to know who or what it is. Pay attention to which part you are identifying with. If you are watching the world from the viewpoint of your transcendent observer, you will feel peacefully detached from the events of your life, knowing they do not define who you are. If you are feeling angst, worry, frustration, edginess, judgmental, and just "not enough," then you are identifying with the story of your life and your small self is in the driver's seat.

Place your hands on your heart and say to yourself, "Just for today, I will activate my transcendent observer and watch the story of my life unfold. I will watch with love, with curiosity, and pay attention to how I feel." If you are having a particularly challenging moment, repeat this activity and say, "just for this moment . . ." instead of "just for today." Start with just a moment and work up to a day. With practice, the transcendent observer will become easier to identify and to connect with within you.

BECOME A JOY DETECTIVE

During my work in the schools, I have often invited students to become "joy detectives," asking them to not only notice, but to actively look for joy in every day. Most of us have generally been trained to look for what is "wrong"—or the "x" of life—instead of what feels good, or the "o." I believe that we can mind our heart wings by retraining our brains to look for the "o's" of our life and that this expands one's heart wings. These "o's" are the clues to what animates, what brings more energy into your system instead of depleting it. The more you live from your heart, the more you can live with ease, with grace, and with less resistance.

Here are some ways to become a joy detective today:

1. Count your blessings. Pause and celebrate when you find one. Place your hands on your heart and honor it. Really acknowledge it and feel the associated feelings inside when you hold this blessing in your heart and mind.

2. Start a gratitude journal. Gratitude is a practice that directs your awareness toward the "o's" of your life. I love the Gratitude Journal app, by the Happy Tapper, found in the Apple iTunes store. I downloaded it on my phone so that I can collect my items of gratitude easily during my day. This practice of gratitude creates a reverence for the life you presently have, giving you a starting point for minding your wings, for caring and nurturing your heart.

3. Create a magical journal to record the things that enliven and ignite your interest throughout the day. My journal is black paper and I collect the magic with metallic pens. Make it fun!

SATURATE, ANIMATE, RADIATE

SATURATE: Surround yourself with positive energy. Be mindful of what you are listening to or who you are hanging out with. Notice if the overarching tones are positive or negative. If the tone tends to be negative, then do a little shift. Broadcast some positive ideas through the Bluetooth in your car. Watch uplifting movies and listen to uplifting music. Read something that inspires you before bed. Walk in nature. Take a soothing bath by candlelight. Eat a wholesome snack. Saturate your life with the resonance of love.

ANIMATE: Begin to notice what you are drawn to in life. Pay attention to the fluctuation of energy around the things that interest you most. When I feel more positive energy around something, I call it my inner animation because it gives me *more* energy (not less) when I do it. Pause for a moment and consider what you would be doing if you could live your ideal day. Where would you be? Who or what sorts of people would be around you? What activities would fill your life? Next, consider, has there been something you have always wanted to try but haven't yet? Write all these things down in a journal entry. Now begin each day to do at least one thing that animates you, gives you *more* energy when you do it. Have fun!!!

RADIATE: As you begin to saturate and animate and the more you mind your heart wings, you naturally begin to radiate love. Take a moment each day to sit silently for one minute, minimum (more minutes if you feel like it). As you sit and gently breathe in and out, tune in to a small pinpoint of light within you. Watch as that little pinpoint of light grows and expands outward, radiating with the heartbeat of life, with the heartbeat of love. Feel the steady rhythm vibrating within you. See the light expanding from within you out into the space around you. Now see it spreading out into your living and working environments and your community. Watch as it starts to permeate the environment around the world, flowing and expanding out into space. Feel that light vibrating within all your cells. Breathe. You are radiating love, your heart wings are fully expanded, you are filled with light and love. Feel and connect with your heart wings.

CHAPTER 6:

STILLNESS AND SOLITUDE: BUILDING THE BRIDGE

Love is the bridge between you and everything.
~Rumi

I was continuing the long journey from my head to my heart. I've always had a really overactive mind, so this pathway was proving to be a challenge. Regardless, as my heart wings continued to expand and unfold, I was feeling more and more of my heart, and I was determined to stick with it.

In journeying more fully into my heart, two of my new best friends were stillness and solitude. The more time I spent in the company of these friends, the more I began to feel my heart. Up until this point in time, I really hadn't spent much time alone. And all of that focus on other people kept me solidly distracted from myself. To be honest, solitude had been more of an enemy than a friend, hence the chain-dating spree and relationship madness.

When I was in middle school, I can remember the panic attacks that would ensue when my parents began to go out occasionally and leave my sister and me alone at the farmhouse. I had an ingenious imagination that could create all sorts of mayhem out of shadows, creaks, and all other bumps in the noisy, country night. Once, a tree frog landed on the kitchen window and began its sticky crawl up the screen. You would've thought a grenade had gone off the way my nervous system responded. My nervous system was in constant overdrive, set in default to the "on" position, ready for any sign of danger or sudden change in the environment around me. When I spotted the tree frog, a protective cascade of adrenaline was unleashed in my body; my heart pounded and I was short of breath. My neighbor friend jumped in to attempt to distract my anxious mind out of its frantic, reactive pattern. She told jokes and offered snacks, but to no avail.

My first real experiment with sustained solitude came when I studied abroad in Granada, Spain, during my final undergraduate semester. Being thousands of miles across the sea and in a foreign culture, complete with a language barrier, forced me to learn to do deep breathing to calm myself. I was still drowning in constant panic and anxiety, at this time in my life, however. I spent my twenty-first birthday alone, climbing the majestic forested pathways that led up to the Alhambra, a magnificent palace of thirty-seven towers that took the Moors over 150 years to build. The

Alhambra, whose name means in Arabic, "the red one," is a UNESCO World Heritage Site and considered to be one of the top wonders of the world. Inside this castle, teeming with romance and mystery, I walked the arabesque hallways and gardens. Surrounded by the delicate Arabic designs of mocárabe, a complex array of prisms cast in plaster that emulates stalactites, I felt inspiration bubbling in my own cells. The Moors considered gardens to be symbols of paradise on earth and these gardens felt as such. Inspiration surely graced author, historian, and diplomat Washington Irving as he inhabited one of the castle rooms for a time in the 1820s, long enough to dive into the history, converse with the inhabitants, and gather research for his *Tales of the Alhambra*, one of his literary masterpieces.

I walked the gardens and took in the reflection pools. A teacher of mine in Spain explained in a Spanish art class that the Moors designed reflection pools to symbolize the unification of the material world and the world of the Divine; an "as above, so below" sort of connotation. I loved this explanation and used to reflect, myself, on how the microcosms of life mirror the greater macrocosm of the universe at large.

Feeling the magic, the romance of the place, listening to faint guitar lullabies drifting up from beyond the stone walls, gazing out at the glow of tea houses tucked within the stone caves of the gypsy quarter, I felt in awe of the beauty that is so wonderfully individualized and expressed throughout the world. While I wasn't technically alone in this solitude, as I was surrounded by tourists milling about, I was somehow wrapped in a divine stillness, and I sampled my own creation of magical moments that were growing from within me. It was here that I began to understand the power of the pilgrimage. I realized that traveling to an unfamiliar destination could be a tool I used to catapult myself into the awareness of my senses and connection to the world around me. In dropping myself into a foreign place, free of usual duty and distraction, I was suddenly ultra-present with each molecule within and around me.

I captured the Alhambra experience so completely that now, as I am typing, I am transported back to that moment. I can feel the dampness in the air, the coolness of the shadow of the trees, and the coldness of the stone of the *Puerta de las Granadas*, Gate of the Pomegranates, which I entered to begin my exploration of the castle grounds. These feelings are present now as I write these words twenty-two years later because I allowed myself total mindfulness as I explored that day up on the mount. I still keep an ink drawing of the Alhambra's Court of the Lions on the wall in my house to remind me of these first delicate glimpses. When I was at the Alhambra, the distinction between me and the outside world blurred, much like the mirror image of the reflective pools in front of the palaces, and I was fully mindful of each detail, each nuance of beauty. These details brought me deeper into my own soul.

I'm not advocating that you trek the Himalayas to find your hermit cave dwelling or buy a cabin "off the grid" to seek your soul, although those methods certainly work for some. Not all of us can just hightail it off to the desert for years on end, or even days. What I *am* suggesting is that you carve out specific moments to free yourself from the distraction of others so that you can listen to and be present with your soul.

I have a dear friend, a kindred spirit, who works a somewhat stressful job in information technology (IT). Every week, on Wednesdays, she takes what she calls a "mid-week weekend" with herself. She closes the door, soaks in a candlelit bath, or simply sits alone, being with her soul, to rejuvenate for a few hours. She's a mom and is taking time to be with her beautiful self, to activate her awareness of her heart in the middle of her workweek.

As for myself, as a mom—a single mom—and mostly "only parent" to boot, I couldn't just drop everything and head for the hills, as much as I wanted to at times. I could have, I suppose, since anything is possible, but I didn't *want* to. So, in my dating pause, I decorated a quiet corner in my bedroom where I seduced my spirit every day and relished a few drops of silence. I was determined to heed Jesus' invitation to "enter into thy closet" (Matthew 6:6, King James Version) and close the door to seek what St. Teresa of Avila hailed as the "interior castle" of her soul. So, by and by, early morning became my refuge, when I spent time with my soul. In that self-created cave, with stillness and solitude, I touched my heart and learned to be quiet and to listen deeply.

Through the Keyhole-Shaped Doorway

In this stillness and solitude, I began to explore my interior world. After reading St. Teresa's *Interior Castle*, I thought about my own interior castle, my soul, and decided that it was a lot like the Alhambra. The Alhambra was known as a "pearl set in emeralds" due to the white/reddish coloring of the buildings set within the lush, dense green of the surrounding forest. Each entrance to the castle was graced with a doorway shaped like a keyhole. I love the elegance and the gracefulness of these magical doorways! My heart, I found, was much the same. In the stillness and solitude, it was as if I was peeking through a doorway to enter my heart, the pearl of wisdom nestled within the lush, green garden of my soul.

Green has long been associated with the heart chakra. It is the color of growth and life. As I sat in that stillness, I felt new life begin to bloom within me, an animation of my spirit that started to spark to life. In their book *Microchakras*, Sri Shyamji Bhatnagar and Dr. David Isaacs discuss the presence of a smaller microchakra within the heart chakra known as hreta padma, which means *lotus of the heart* in Sanskrit. In this inner sanctuary, "The Divine Self swells in profound silence within each of us." Interesting . . . here it was again. Through silence, we access the heart. By embracing stillness and solitude, I was delving deeper into my heart center, where I found this animation of life that I call my Shangri-Love. Just like the brilliant key-hole shaped doorways of ancient Islamic art, stillness and solitude brought me deeper into my own presence.

LOTUS OF THE HEART

Have you heard that saying, "No mud, no lotus"? Since ancient time, the heart has been likened to a lotus flower. An ancient text, the Chandogya Upanishad, referred to the heart as a lotus flower. Buddha himself detailed the lotus sutras, instructions for bringing people more into heart-centered awareness. The flower of life, also known as the seed of life, is an ancient symbol that has been found in civilizations around the world, from Egypt to China. It's in a phyllotaxis pattern, the same design found in a blooming lotus.

One could say that the flowering of the heart lotus is a flowering of consciousness within the heart, or thinking from the heart. I once wrote a children's meditation called "the flower within you" and at the time I was imagining my heart as a lotus flower, slowly blooming from the various muds of my life. As I spent time in stillness and solitude, I felt the petals of my heart open wider. Each bump along the way of life, however, threatened to knock me off course and pull my attention back into my head, away from my heart. Those times are what Caroline Myss refers to as "divine chaos" and, if accepted fully, can be the grace that opens our heart even more, expanding our capacity to love rather than shutting it down. An opening of the heart is the ideal scenario, and yet the tendency in the face of pain is to close down, close off, and retreat. It sometimes feels like grace may be the only power that can shift a string of chaotic life events and expand us rather than contract us.

Often, I think we experience both an expansion *and* a contraction. They work in collaboration to more fully open our heart lotus. The more we simply meet and be with what "is," the more we are "bloomed" by grace, by love, by the Divine. As with the burning of my condo, these moments of intense fear or intense unknown can be the catalysts for deeper blooming, for deepening into the heart, and for working the petals open in the face of an extreme challenge.

During this period, some days I woke up and felt less than inspired, "In Spirit." I felt as if I was in my own way, the old voices of fear and doubt and self-loathing threatening my inner peace. In those moments, I returned to stillness and solitude. I went to the cave of my heart to touch grace, reaching for the divine drink of my soul that sustained me and deepened my growth. What I came to know is that the sooner I hit the meditation cushion, the sooner I began to commune with my inner heart lotus.

As I meditated with my heart, the lotus of my heart petals began to unfold, to expand, and to grow. These petals grew with the waters of compassion, the gentleness of surrender and with deeper trust of the Divine. Within this beautiful, silent, dark cave within my heart, I found Shangri-Love. In this place I sourced the nectar of my soul, and I touched my union with all life. Joy radiated from within this place. And all was completely peaceful and at ease. All was well with the universe. In the quietness there, I felt the spark of love and a subtle energetic flow with just a touch of bliss. This was the elixir of life, and I sensed the stuff from which EVERYTHING arises, back to that flower of life again! In this wonderment of my soul, I felt the magical union of my heart and my mind. Actually, it felt as if the mind simply quieted down and the heart was just a state of presence. The more I spent time in this space, the more it became easily accessible to me. What a contrast from my previous dating in Neverland, where I was constantly stressed, tense, and felt as if I never touched love for more than a millisecond. Now I was experiencing a more sustainable joy, and I was finding it inside me!

FOOT OFF THE ACCELERATOR

Slowing down to access stillness and solitude was *not* as easy as it is to type here. I entered this world with my foot on the accelerator. Born seven weeks premature, I was always one step ahead of my own self. Nothing moved fast enough for me as a child or as an adult. And what eventually transpired from my need for speed was that I lived my life at full throttle and didn't slow down much. This resulted in a high level of anxiety, adrenal fatigue, and an overall state of exhaustion.

I was a highly anxious child, and my oldest daughter, Maiya, inherited this tendency from me. Her struggles with anxiety, which eventually led to obsessive-compulsive disorder (OCD), were the inspiration for my creation of the blog at kidsrelaxation.com. I delighted in finding ways to make relaxation fun and engaging for kids, and slowly the ideas spread around the world. I would hear from teachers and therapists from Mexico to New Zealand, Ireland to Turkey.

While Maiya used long-distance running and intellectual pursuits to be her ways to channel and embrace the excess energy of anxiety and calm down, I continued to experiment with various forms of meditation, bodywork, and energy work, both for kids and for myself. I searched for a way to give my nervous system a break. I was intent on learning how to relax, how to let go, and my overactive mind was intent on keeping me hostage in an Amazon jungle of thought.

My anxiety surfaced in the stillness of my morning meditation time and I began to experience a torrent of emotion. Memories, both positive and negative, would seemingly pop into my mind out of nowhere. Some days I was so antsy and anxious that I hastily sat and then hurried on to the distractions of my day. I would think thoughts such as—*How hard can this really be? Just sit here and relax.* But I was filled with wiggle! Other days, I would sit and attempt to be present with all that was coming forth. I soon learned that the more I was able to just allow whatever I wanted to happen to happen, the more peaceful I felt inside and the longer I was able to sit. One hundred percent acceptance was totally necessary.

It was as Adyashanti teaches on his meditation CDs, titled *True Meditation*. He explains that meditation is starting from the place of allowing everything to "be as it is, that we start from the natural state at the beginning, rather than moving toward or trying to create the natural state." He suggests that "we let go of the meditator, the controller, and to sit down and allow everything to be as it is." He further explains that there is "nothing to attain and that a sense of peace comes from allowing everything in our experience to just *be*." This is what I experienced as well.

What occurred to me was that the more I could just allow the wiggle, and the more I could meet everything with the essence of "okay" (which is my version of allowing and acceptance), the more I would feel peaceful inside. One morning an image of me walking around in a dark, parking lot at my childhood church came to mind. While I watched this memory take form, I saw that I was walking in circles and then I realized that it was the evening of my sister's birth! It had just finished raining and it was Halloween. I had been trick-or-treating for UNICEF with my church and was waiting for my grandparents.

Now, memories are foggy and often extrapolated through the filter of other memories faded with time, but this is what came forward. I was four years old and wearing a blue, fluffy jacket over my Halloween costume. Walking around in the puddles, I was filled with worry. What would it be like to be a big sister? What would she be like? But the sense that stuck with me now, in meditation, was the worry, would I continue to be special? Would I now have to share my parents with someone else, and would that somehow make me less important? This was the important nugget coming forward for me in present adult-ville. Sitting with those feelings, I began to talk with that little worried girl. I assured her that I would take care of her now and that she was special and important. Those were the words that she was yearning to hear. In the silence and stillness, I touched a place in my heart that was unsure, a shadow where I still wondered if I mattered, if I was cared for. This heart place now got a big dose of love and was able to let go, in love.

As I sat, I started to develop and cultivate a neutrality of being, which seeped out into daily life. Even though I wasn't always able to access this neutral feeling of benevolence when life bumps happened, I shortened the period of time it took to return to a calm place. Another "friend" that helped me bring this about was mindfulness.

SUPERHERO ATTENTION: MINDFULNESS

One of my more popular blogs at kidsrelaxation.com was about Spiderman and his mindfulness skills. He possessed the abilities of super hearing, super touch, and super seeing, much like a spider. In his ultra-awareness of his senses, he was ultra-mindful of the world around him. Kids love to learn Spiderman mindfulness!!

Mindfulness was key to me generating my ability to be present with myself, within myself, as I learned to live in stillness. Because I wasn't dating, I had freed up more time to just be present and to practice being mindful. This mindfulness, or being fully attentive in the present moment, allowed me greater and greater contact with my heart, with the Shangri-Love within me. Thich Nhat Hanh teaches in his book, *True Love: A Practice for Awakening the Heart*, that, "in Buddhism, the energy that helps us to touch life deeply is called *smrti*, the energy of mindfulness. Everyone, he continues, possesses a seed (*bija*) of this energy."

I had several tools that helped me to be fully present, in tune with my heart, at home with myself. One of them, a bit unbelievable, was my big, yellow, cruiser bike. I got on that beautiful, bright yellow bike, complete with yellow tires and a big basket up front, and I entered a world of presence. As I rode, I tuned in to all the details passing me by, allowing them to make themselves known to me, receiving all the beauty around me. I took in the breeze on my face, the dewdrops on each grass frond, the illumination of the spider's web, wet from the early morning rain, breathing deeply the richness of the morning air. I allowed my senses free rein, hitting the pause button on my thoughts. I simply absorbed what *was* present: the birds chattering back and forth; the bunny racing through the field of prairie dogs. And soon, a whole new world opened up before me! I noticed things that had previously blended in to the background of my thinking world. And in those moments I felt the energy of God awake in all my cells, bringing goosebumps to my arms and vibrant chills running throughout my nervous system. It was like the world became Technicolor by my witnessing it!

Another way I awakened mindfulness was through my binoculars. I opened to the eternally big world that was present through the end of the lens. Looking out from my porch,

I found universes in the neighborhood trees. I can't fathom what the neighbors must have thought of me sitting with my binoculars peering into the trees, but the world just became infinitely larger and magnificently explorable from the comfort of my porch swing.

Finally, I took pictures of flowers to practice looking deeply into the world around me. I imagined crawling within the petals and taking in every minute detail of the world within the flower. Much like my own heart and your own heart, the infinity of life exists within us. This flower, this looking deeply, showed me the keyhole into me. It was like training my brain to go within and being truly present to the beauty inside.

THE TRANSCENDENT OBSERVER

In being present in my heart and tuning in to Shangri-Love, I was able to activate my transcendent observer, the witness of my thoughts *even more*. Just as I discussed in Chapter Five, this transcendent observer continued to bring more freedom to my life. More and more, my awareness deepened in understanding that the "storyline" of my life was not WHO I was, it was WHAT was happening in my life. The more I sat in stillness, the more I became the watcher, the transcendent observer of my life, and the less resistance I had to the events to my life. If I was no longer the story, no longer the chain dater, no longer the princess incessantly hunting a prince, then I was this BEING, this Shangri-Love instead. Whew! That was a relief!

What's more, being the observer gave me enough space from the story to have even more power to change it, if I desired. Or, I could simply watch it unfold, much like a movie on the screen. Being Shangri-Love rather than the story, I detached from the outcomes much more easily. In this stillness and silence, letting go and allowing my thoughts to be free, I was a presence and an essence, rather than the forms circulating around me, such as my bank account, or the events that made up the story of my life. I was much more than all that.

HEARTMATH

This "much more"—or essence and presence—bloomed from what the HeartMath® Institute terms "coherence." I continued to refine the bridge between my heart and mind through stillness, solitude, meditation, and mindfulness practice. I experienced more and more coherence, what I felt when my mind and heart were working in collaboration. Coherence is a state of well-being that is born from a well-established bridge of communication between your heart and mind.

The HeartMath Institute is a research firm that has dedicated decades of research to the heart's resonance, or the electromagnetic field surrounding the heart, and found it to be a generator of energy, a brilliant broadcasting station, nearly sixty times larger than that of the electromagnetic field of the brain! HeartMath has also coined the term "heart coherence," which describes the nature of heart/brain/body balance within the body.

Based on the knowledge that is growing out of the institute's research, we have just tapped the surface of the intelligence of the heart. The research is determining that the heart is intuitive, that it can sense happenings before they are even within the brain's awareness. On the HeartMath website, heart coherence is referred to as the state of being where your heart rhythm pattern is in a coherent mode, producing a physiological and emotional state of alignment, and a deep feeling of well-being is achieved.

Coherence was originally a term used in physics to mean the orderly distribution of energy in waveform. Using biofeedback technology, scientists at HeartMath measured heart rate variability in individuals who were practicing certain exercises to balance the heart/brain/body communication. Biofeedback technology is a set of sensors and/or instruments that connect an individual to a computer and provide real time information as to the physiological functions taking place. The goal is for individuals to increase awareness of how they are impacting these physiological functions, such as heart rate or skin conductance or temperature, at will, and to increase health and well-being as a result. Biofeedback teaches people to increase their ability to impact physiological functions with practice and attention. When an individual achieved a state of coherence, the heart rate variance showed up in sine waves, fluid, balanced, and even-flowing waves. When a person was in distress, such as in a state of anxiety, depression, or extreme fear, the heart waves were choppy, erratic, jagged—there was little coherence. The scientist concluded that coherence means "clarity of thought, emotional balance, and the quality of being orderly, consistent, and intelligible."

I became trained as a HeartMath practitioner because I found so much value in the HeartMath tools. The tools have a high rate of success in reducing anxiety, depression, and even attention deficit disorder (ADD). I have used these tools for years with myself and with children in the public school system. One tool I especially like that helps me to "lock in" feelings of joy is the "Heart Lock-In®." This technique involves pausing for a moment to place your attention on the area of your heart and to simultaneously connect with feelings of gratitude within yourself while breathing deeply. As events unfold throughout the day, I continue to check in and repeat this quick technique to return to "being in my heart."

The slowing down, stillness, and solitude truly deepened my experience of my heart, but my need for speed still hadn't quite calmed down all the way. At times, this Shangri-Love experience was in danger of feeling a little bit like a holding tank. I would need another key in order to continue to unlock my journey. I felt like I still lacked acceptance for the way my life was and in this resistance, I was staying stuck. To be still is a shock to the mind that wants to "move" things and to "do" all the time. This being in stillness brought an awareness that I continued to struggle with accepting myself exactly as I was. To work through the struggle, I would need to cultivate more self-compassion. That would be the next leg of my journey.

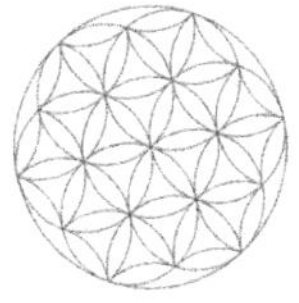

Shangri-Love
Mindfulness Activities:
GET SUPER PRESENT
AND HIT THE PAUSE BUTTON

The past and the future do not create—it is impossible. Therefore, let go of the past (what happened), and let go of the future (what might happen), and devote yourself fully to the present moment and what you are being/doing right here, right now. This is mindfulness practice. Your energy is most powerful when it is presently focused. To think of what things used to be like or might be like scatters your energy and dilutes your present creation. Pull your attention into now and connect with your deep heartfelt presence. This creates abundance—deep fulfilling abundance—right now. Celebrate now. Be present now. Act from NOW.

Set aside several times throughout your day where you can truly pause, turn off the phone, and just breathe and tune in to what is going on within you. Pick an activity that you do automatically every day and tune in during that activity. For example, every time you do the dishes, stop and take a few mindful breaths. See if you can connect with the bubbles on your hands and really feel them. Notice the water droplets on the pans. Just observe without judgment. Allow your senses to bring you fully into the present. Allow yourself to BE.

MINDFULNESS PRACTICES I LOVE

Take a mindfulness bike ride. While you are on the ride, drink in every sensation that you can. See if you can feel the air on your skin and what it feels like when you breathe it in. Notice the feeling of your feet on the pedals. See if you can pause along the way and study a blade of grass. Listen to every sound as if each one is falling separately into your ears. Breathe deeply as you ride slowly. Feel as if you are totally alive in the present moment, totally in tune with every delightful sense that is being awakened by your ride.

Practice thirty minutes of mindfulness photography. Make your world infinitely smaller by pausing to photograph the insides of flowers. Imagine that you are a bee or a butterfly and you are crawling inside the flower to get a totally new perspective. Capture each small part possible. See how many parts you can photograph individually.

CHAPTER 7:

THE SACRED KEY: SELF-COMPASSION

I loved my newfound stillness and solitude. I was touching my heart and feeling so good inside, but at the same time, I was afraid. Yes, I was deathly afraid of being left behind. What if all of life kept moving and I drowned in this quicksand of trying to improve myself? What if I woke up someday and life had passed me by while I was trying to be still and alone? My ADD brain, so used to having someone else to focus on, so used to doing something at all times, began to struggle, and took a detour down Wanting Things to Be Different Quickly Lane! "Quickly" was the key word. "Okay, I've practiced stillness and solitude, now what?"

I was also sliding back into the muck of self-imposed victimhood. I wondered things like, "Why hasn't my life panned out like I originally planned?" and "What if I take some time here to find myself and I never return to my creative life?" Oh, how the mind stealthily wanted to take over once again.

It didn't help matters that my stillness and solitude had given me a newfound energy for life. I loved the energy, of course! But with it came a feeling of inspiration, which is a natural by-product of deep stillness. This was tricky. Since my head had been used to running the show, it got a glimpse of the new idea candy and would quickly take over and return me to busy thought, planning, and action taking. I went into my default mode of overthinking and overdoing.

Around and around I would go with the "next great idea" or the "next way to make myself better." I studied with many a business coach eager to whip my entrepreneurial mindset into shape. I was drawn to many a glittery mastermind that promised to get me on the right track to Entre-preneur-ville.

I filled up journals with ideas for creation. Just as I would start on one idea, another would snag my attention. I would get on the next fancy horse and ride in another direction, and then another and another. I had so many horses! Instead of creating anything, I created a little bit of everything and finished nothing. I got stuck chasing my creativity tail. Oh the stress of distraction!

My mind was cluttered with a crazy ADD universe of creative projects: shelves and shelves of entrepreneurial ideas, websites, children's games, CDs, books, cards, activities, workshops, classes, and speeches and books waiting to be written. My frenzy of creativity and unrealized projects reflected a lingering self-aversion. It was disguised as self-improvement and self-change, other distractors on the road to Shangri-Love. If I wasn't careful, I would replace dating with creating. From the space I was in, creating was still stressful. Rather than carrying with it the energy of love, it still reeked of fear. I still wasn't enough, regardless. Now, I was attempting to be enough through creative endeavors as opposed to measuring myself by the Prince Charming on my arm. In riding all these creativity horses, I was well intentioned, and yet I was getting ahead of myself.

See, the horse I was really yearning for and wanting to ride was self-compassion. This was the horse that would lead me deeper into Shangri-LOVE. As I continued to return to the meditation mat, this became clearer. It was time to take a deeper dive into the application of self-compassion, but I wasn't exactly sure what that meant. How did I do it? What was the recipe? With the assistance of several brilliant teachers, I began to figure out what it meant for me.

One Hundred Percent Acceptance

First stop on the self-compassion train—100 percent acceptance. Remember the mean girl from Chapter Four? Facing up to her started me on the path of learning how to gently accept myself. With 100 percent acceptance, I was going to continue on that path. Now it was time to practice it with more and more of my life. Like a cloud thinning and spreading out to fill the sky, I was going to expand the practice of acceptance in my life.

One hundred percent acceptance had little to do with liking the way things are or even condoning what was happening and had everything to do with allowing things to be as they are. Furthermore, it meant accessing and cultivating a neutrality within me *to be able to* accept things the way they are.

Being able to accept the world at large without resistance is the first half of the 100 percent acceptance; the second half is being to accept ourselves the way we are. These two paths of acceptance are strengths that are honed and polished over time. This ability to accept ourselves and the world around us "as is" is often referred to as nonresistance. How is it that we build this essence of neutrality, this non-resistance? I believe it is through continued letting go and purification of the heart center.

First, by accepting ourselves exactly the way we are, we build this essence of neutrality toward ourselves. Then, I believe, much like an internal bank account of acceptance, we are able to transfer this neutrality to accepting others and the world outside ourselves as they/it are.

I found a reference manual on self-acceptance in Tara Brach's book, *Radical Acceptance: Embracing Your Life with the Heart of a Buddha,* and the corresponding CD. Oh, what a balm for my soul I found in her teachings. In her discussions she addresses what she calls a "pervasive type of contemporary suffering" that includes "pervasive feelings of not okay and not enough." She explains, "Our path is to not reject any part of our life" and gently guides us, through her practices and teachings, to "re-embrace the parts of life that have been excluded."

In thinking about self-acceptance, I realized that when I rejected parts of my life, my heart would close to these parts. For example, I would get so upset with myself when I watched how attached I was to pleasing others. I would go around work smiling and "trying" to be the best school psychologist, but sometimes I didn't feel aligned with the smile on my face. As a school psychologist working with students with significant needs, it was often necessary to ask teachers and other school staff to provide interventions or support that was difficult to do. My requests often weren't popular and I would turn that on myself personally. I would also worry about whether my team liked me, if the students were learning in my groups, and that I might not be doing a good job. All this worry created stuck energy, which was like sticky residue around my heart. The more residue I had, the quicker I was to be triggered and to experience strong, unpleasant emotions. I would be more judgmental of others, which at a deeper level was just a projection of judgments I was having about myself. All of this residue was getting in the way of my connection with my heart center, that essence of well-being I call Shangri-Love.

I found that a powerful way to clear the residue (because residue happens) around my heart was to acknowledge my feelings. At first I found this difficult because of my spirituality. You see, society tends to promote the idea that unwanted feelings and so-called "negative energy" are not spiritual. Unwanted feelings are seen as "wrong" and we are taught to avoid them at all costs. This closes down the heart to "what is." I have struggled with this so much! In an effort to appear healed and positive, it's easy for me to overlook my genuine feelings that *are* present. I've had to learn to stop and acknowledge my sadness, or anger, or suspicion—and then move toward the light. You see, my soul knows either way. It knows when I am feeling something, and it knows when I am ignoring that feeling. And the more I ignore or pretend, the more stuck energy bottles up and comes out sideways later on. Learning to fully accept "what is" means accepting the pleasant *and* the not so pleasant.

After acknowledgment, then what do we do with the stuff we've acknowledged? Brach teaches that our "essential nature is good, we are love." As I immersed myself in these teachings, I began to do what Ernest Holmes, founder of the International Religious Science movement and author of *The Science of Mind,* identified as "turning away from conditions." Through deeper contemplation, I began to shift away from "something is wrong with me that needs fixing" to a deeper sense of self-worth born of "my essential nature is good, I am love." See the difference? The most basic foundation of me was love instead of flaw. This had a powerful relaxation effect on my life.

Brach's teachings peeled off the layers of residue clouding my heart until I could reach what she refers to as "shame: the etymological root of belief that we are fundamentally flawed." This was the juice fueling my incessant need to continually improve myself, to do it better, to achieve more. As a result of false interpretations and fear-based perceptions, I believed I was fundamentally flawed in some way. I could soothe myself away from this belief to a certain degree (by reminding myself that "I am love"), but I needed to get to the root of it to make a sustained difference.

Again and again, with the application of self-compassion, self-acceptance allowed the parts of myself that I viewed as flawed back into the wholeness of myself. So when I began to judge myself at work as not good enough, I would turn it around and begin with "I'm doing the best I can in this moment" instead. And, if I found that I didn't believe I was doing the best I could, then I would ask myself what sort of steps I could take to do it differently. In this way, I began to transform the idea that I wasn't good enough as a school psychologist into the knowledge that my work was heart-driven, and that would serve the children well.

RESPONDING WITH LOVE

About this time, my life coach, Seran, was teaching me about the "essence of okay." If I could truly and deeply embrace this essence and energy of "okay," then I would be free of the energy I was expending, trying, in vain, to change and control the world around me. I did this through continually asking myself the question, *If I really accepted this, then . . . ?* By asking this question, I was letting go and shifting to the present moment. My feelings became my greatest signals, the litmus test of where I was in any given moment. If I felt stressed, overwhelmed, scared, or any other sort of discomfort, then that was the clue that somewhere inside I was resisting either a belief about myself or a belief about the world.

This essence of okay meant unconditional love. I was learning how to show myself compassion. Seran was equating love with the practice of telling myself, "I see you and I accept you just as you are." Once again, it didn't mean that I necessary liked whatever it was that was going on, but it meant that I accepted it, that I was no longer pushing against it. Like when I would have an argument with one of my daughters, instead of cascading into thoughts of *this shouldn't be happening,* or *I'm a terrible parent* or *I am overwhelmed and all alone,* I would state that I was frustrated, leave the room, and go to breathe and relax my mind so that I could reconnect with my heart and consider my options, ones that would allow for more love and peace. Just as muscles strengthen with resistance, I knew that what I resisted got stronger. Therefore, through letting go, I was allowing myself a beautiful space through which to view the situation and decide how to respond. *Okay, now what . . .* became my mantra and my saving grace from a whole lot of tension and arguments with LIFE.

PERMISSION TO FALL

Another side effect of allowing life to "be as it is" was that I gave myself permission to fall down. As Seran said, "Life is not about not falling down, it is about what you do when you do fall down and how quickly you get back up." Falling down is a part of life and it is inevitable. Fear says that we must avoid challenge at all cost, avoid falling down at all cost. Love says that falling down is part of the path. If you love your way into and through it without avoiding the pain, you allow your heart to open in the face of adversity. With this newfound freedom, when I fell down, I was beginning to activate kindness, gentleness, and understanding with myself. It wasn't that I wasn't still growing and expanding in awareness, just that now I was allowing myself the practice time!

See, all these years, I'd done battle with this little thing called perfectionism. Remember all those creative ideas I discussed earlier in the chapter? Well, one reason that those ideas never made it to fruition, and were a constant source of stress, was that they weren't, in my eyes . . . perfect. I'm not going to write because it's not . . . perfect. I won't sing because it's not . . . perfect. I won't get on stage because my speech may not come out . . . perfect. Also, I shout a BIG NO to painting, drawing, dancing in public, yoga-ing, because I can't do the poses like a yogini, or marketing my products. Nope, I will be having none of any of that! All these creative projects just didn't measure up to the brilliance in my head, and I was quick to abandon them if they didn't come out the way I wanted the first time I created them. Maybe you have felt the same and stifled some of your creativity too. Perfectionism can be a prison sentence to a life under-lived and under-shared and certainly closes down the heart along the way.

There's a quote from Zenmaster Dogen that says, "To be in the harmony with the oneness of things is to be without anxiety about imperfection." This speaks to me of the perfection of imperfection. What if everything is already perfect the way it is? If it exists, God sanctioned it for some grand reason. If I was to bask in the joy of Shangri-LOVE, then this obsessive perfectionism that kept me paralyzed in life had to go. I think Elizabeth Gilbert sums up the energy of perfectionism with her quote from the book *Big Magic*, "Perfectionism is just fear in fancy shoes and a mink coat." That quote tickles me. Yes, perfectionism is a clever smoke screen of fear to hide behind, to keep you small. It was linked to my shame and my idea that what I had to share with the world wasn't good enough.

Self-compassion was the key to working through my perfectionism. I was no longer resisting the fall-down, and I was focusing on being gentle and loving as I was getting up. This shift of focus was the ultimate permission to live life full out, and with that, my heart was relaxing more and more into Shangri-Love.

PENNILESS IN PARIS

The cool thing about working on self-compassion is that life immediately responds with ways to practice.

One of the great gifts of my parenting life was when I was able to arrange and pay for a vacation with my girls in France. One year in November, I was having tea with a good friend who was telling me about her upcoming trip to Italy to celebrate her anniversary with her husband. As she was describing a divine-sounding planned visit to the city of Lucca, a tiny seed started forming in my mind. Wouldn't it be beyond a dream to be able to take my girls to Paris? It had been on their vision boards for years, ever since I painted an oddly abstract version (not intentionally abstract, mind you) of the Eiffel Tower on my daughter's bedroom wall when she was four. After my tea with that friend, I joined another friend for lunch in a neighboring town. Just as I was about to share the seed that had just been planted, she said, "You know, my partner and I are going to France next spring on a business trip and you and your girls are welcome to join us if you would like." At this, my mouth literally fell open. I was stunned. This was like instant manifestation! Spirit had just watered my seed and turned it into a little sprout, a sure sign that the girls and I were going to France.

Over the next six months, I carefully planned and pre-paid for plane tickets, accommodations, and excursions within France. I wanted the least amount of stress possible so that we could fully enjoy and be present while we were there, shopping, touring, and eating as we would like within a carefully planned, stress-free budget. We bought travel books and sticky-noted the highlights that each of us wanted to see. As the trip neared, we prepared our wardrobes. The girls showed me how to "take a selfie" of my various outfits for the trip so that I would not over pack and would have an "outfit menu" of sorts to dress myself while traveling. We modeled for one another and excitedly packed our bags. I even splurged on an Italian leather wallet, feeling as if I would fit in and look super "European-stylish-like" carrying my money (usually I deemed purses and wallets to be rather extravagant). I was also studying the concepts of financial manifestation and felt like I was sending a message to my subconscious that I was caring for my money with thoughtfulness and love.

The day of our departure finally came and we jetted over the ocean, stopping to briefly see the exotic, foreign terrain of Iceland on the way. We embarked on our journey of love into the ultimate city of art and creativity. Paris does not disappoint. We were enraptured by her beauty and walked miles and miles exploring the Paris neighborhoods, or *arrondissements*. We drank thick, rich chocolate with real, whipped cream at Angelina's, we traipsed through the side streets in Montmartre to a haberdashery shop filled to the rafters with tassels, button, and vintage silk ribbons. Although we visited most of the "usual spots," it was important to me that the girls have the opportunity to drink in the essence of the city, to capture a genuine glimpse behind the scenes of tourism. But as is the habit of vacation, we did pack a little too much into our final day. We were trying to fit in all the last dangling desires before we caught a train to the south of France the next day. In doing so, we exhausted our feet. Knowing we'd scheduled a bike tour by night and boat ride along the Seine that evening, I stopped by the ATM to plan ahead for both the bike ride and the train ride early the next morning. I hastily stuffed the wad of Euros into the bulging Italian wallet and boarded the Metro. When we sat, Maddie's feet were on their last leg, so to speak, so I bent over to help relieve her pain.

Getting off the subway to walk back to the hotel, it suddenly felt as if my purse was not on my arm. Looking down, it was there, but it was gaping open, completely void of the bulging Italian wallet. Stolen! In my haste, I probably hadn't even closed the zipper and now someone was enjoying the $500 cash and all my credit cards . . . save one loose card lying at the bottom of my purse. A true blessing was this one card.

The girls and I were in shock. And a bit panicked. We frantically looked around the train platform but to no avail. It was gone. The beautiful wallet was gone and there was virtually nothing we could do about it. I felt sick to my stomach. Our beautiful vacation, tarnished! A swarm of thoughts threatened to invade my brain. In talking to the police, they said that most likely it was in a trash can, that thieves generally only wanted the cash.

I knew this was another essential parenting moment. How I responded to this "crisis" would be etched in the girls' minds forever. I hit the pause button, feeling a bit numb and scared, and we walked in silent fear back to the hotel. The one last credit card was an American Express and not everyone accepted that card abroad. My first thought was canceling all those cards. At the hotel desk, however, they wouldn't allow me to call the international numbers since I couldn't pay for it. I didn't know the pin number for cash advances on the card. So, we were effectively penniless in Paris. I had no way to get cash until we met our friends in the south of France the next day. Luckily, I had prepurchased our train tickets!

That night, as we rode bikes on our prepaid tour through the streets of Paris, I attempted not to fret. I tried to let go. This was the perfect time to practice allowing life to be as it was, not avoiding my feelings per se, but acknowledging them and moving into problem-solving mode. Now, my first response could have been, and sort of was, "Crazy! Who totes around an Italian wallet full of cash in an open purse with two young dependents in tow? Wouldn't it have been easier, and perhaps more gratifying, to just fill your wallet with money and *give* it away to someone in need? And worse yet, now someone not only has your cash, but also your driver's license, social security card, and a stack of credit cards! Who travels with their original social security card? You KNOW better!" But, applying the art of nonresistance and attempting to model it for my daughters, I shifted the thought to, *Someone must have needed all of that more than us. I might have just gifted them something important. And what a gem of a learning situation for the girls and me.* And then I added some gentle, loving self-talk, keeping with my intention for compassion, *Yes, you made a mistake and could have been more careful. Yes, you were distracted by fatigue and Maddie's pain. You are human!! Getting on with problem solving will help. Continuing to bash yourself with this crazy talk will not. Now get on with it!* This was the modeling of radical self-acceptance; nonresistance to what was happening, and self-compassion. I discussed this with the girls as they scrambled to get their last Euro coins combined for an ice cream to share.

The next morning, I turned to prayer. In my quiet time, I prayed for an angel. I asked God to surround us with love and support as we traveled that day. I prayed for some Euros to show up to help us get some food for the trip on the train.

I tearfully pleaded with the hotel desk to allow me a few more phone calls to cancel the credit cards, but to no avail. They didn't seem to find my predicament at all surprising nor interesting. We muscled up for the long walk to the train, wrestling with our luggage since now we didn't have Euros for a cab. We left the hotel behind and began the journey down the street, headed onward toward the second half of the trip where we were to meet our friends in Avignon. A businessman ran out of the hotel doors and down the street after us. "Mademoiselle," he called in a thick French accent, "I overheard your troubles, and what do you need, here—take all the cash I have, you will be needing something to eat." He emptied out his Euros from his wallet, totaling about fifty US dollars, and put them in my hands. I began to cry. This was the angel I had been praying for and my heart burst open with gratitude. Although we could have made it without the extra money, this allowed us food for the day and a ride to the train station across the city.

While this is an imperfect example of total surrender to Spirit, it was a start for me, and allowed me to share a taste of nonresistance to life with my girls. And, each time you practice, there is a little deposit in the bank account of love; a little more nonresistance muscle to draw on the next time an obstacle pops up on the path of life.

Self-Compassion, Kwan Yin, and the Slow Drip of Love

When I think of compassion, I think of the Chinese Buddhist goddess, Kwan Yin, who is a goddess of compassion, mercy, and love. Embodying the presence of Divine Mother, she is often referred to as the "divine mother of the East" and is known as the "one who hears prayers." Over the years I have often prayed to this presence of Divine Mother Kwan Yin, asking to know, to embody, and to feel more deeply unconditional love for myself and others.

One day as I was doing research for this book, I remembered a Kwan Yin statue that I used to have. It was a beautiful, white porcelain statute that doubled as a fountain. I could fill her with water, turn her upside down, and then water would slowly, slowly drip from a jar in her hand down into the dragon's mouth at her feet. I would often turn her upside down and sit fascinated, watching the slowly dripping water. In a move several years ago, she broke into unrepairable pieces. I threw her away and then forgot about her beauty until now.

In diving deeply into this study of self-compassion, I felt her presence with me. Feeling compelled by this energy of love, I wrote on a sticky note, "get statue of Kwan Yin," wanting her to be present as I wrote about encountering the heart and learning to listen and live from the heart center. I more or less forgot about this note until a couple of months later. I was gazing at the books in the bookstore of my spiritual center, passing time while I waited for an appointment, when I heard a woman enter and begin speaking to the salesperson behind me. "Oh, wow," she said in amazement, "is that a statue of Kwan Yin?" I tried not to obviously turn around to stare. She and the salesperson discussed the statute over the next few minutes. I kept looking straight ahead at the books in front of me, but the sticky note came into my mind and immediately I felt an inner animation stir. I was inexplicably drawn to the statue in the store even before I'd seen it. After a few minutes, the woman left, leaving

the statue behind. I turned, looked up, and encountered THE MOST PERFECT replica of the previous statue I had owned, although this one was twice the size and even more captivatingly beautiful. I instantly bought her, without even looking at her price tag. In that moment, she was destined to come home with me.

Since that time, Kwan Yin has been a part of this book-writing process. It is much like the practice that Jean Shinoda Bolen, MD, talks about in her book, *Goddesses in Everywoman*. In her book she writes about how to activate the presence of goddesses within us in this modern world. Likening it to the practice of women in ancient Greece, who "knew that their vocation or their stage in life placed them under the domin-ion of a particular goddess whom they honored," she en-courages modern women to be mindful that goddesses exist as archetypes and certain tendencies or energies that the goddess represents can be activated to support us in our cre-ative endeavors.

Tapping into goddess energy is a powerful concept. In this modern day, it's easy to forget that the mystical is all around us. I often encourage myself to open my awareness to the worlds beyond my six senses. It is from these worlds that the energy of the mystics, and the energy of the goddess archetypes and other masters, can inspire me. When I want to activate more love, more compassion, more deep understanding within my life, I invoke the energy of Kwan Yin within myself. In fact, as I write today, her statue sits overlooking my laptop. Today, I have placed a bowl and a vase, both filled with roses from my garden, directly in front of the statue, at Kwan Yin's feet. This is an internal honoring. I turn within myself and honor the compassion within me, calling it forward in my awareness, calling it present. I light a candle and I connect with the compassion within me, connect with love, being present with the energy of love. I say a little prayer: "May I write with love, be inspired by love, and feel deep compassion for myself and others." And then . . . I write.

Doreen Virtue, PhD, in her book, *Archangels and Ascended Masters: A Guide to Working and Healing with Divinities and Deities*, includes a chapter on Kwan Yin. In the chapter she connects with the Kwan Yin energy and receives the following message: "Only through a gentle touch is Nirvana revealed." Through the gentle touch of self-compassion, my heart opens.

As I was meditating one morning, watching that ever-so-slow drip of water from Kwan Yin's jar into the mouth of the dragon below, I was struck with a revelation! This is exactly how compassion works in life: as a slow, gentle drip. This drip of compassion, as I apply it to myself, is the love I bring to touch the shadows and dark places within me, the dragons. I don't slay these places with resistance, but accept them in love. As Tara Brach encouraged me to bring those fragmented energies and rejected parts of myself back into my heart with the practice of acceptance, I reintegrated my heart. Compassion was the slow drip that gradually washed away the residues around my heart, clearing it and purifying, making it more accessible to love. The slow, slow drip of compassion—that is our charge. Slowly, as we allow life to be as it is, we embrace all the parts within ourselves. That is love. This process slowly opened the petals of my heart lotus more and more.

So, through a gentle touch, my life was allowed to unfold. I wasn't pushing, rushing, pulling, chasing, or convincing. Through deep mindfulness and compassion, I allowed what was for me to come to me. Contemplating the energy of compassion and practicing compassion deep within myself, I was able to build on this practice. Allowing life to be as it was allowed me to develop a relationship of presence. I was present to what was within me. I was present for what was in the world around me.

I invite you to hit the pause button the next time you run into obstacles and feel like your life has just taken a detour off a cliff. In the pause, allow yourself to gently see how you respond to yourself at the time of impact. Notice what you say to yourself, the thoughts that run through your mind, where your attention is placed, and how you feel inside. Take a step back from the events, step out of the story of your life, and get a grand perspective of what is truly present. How we treat ourselves when we fall down is the absolute key to the abundance found in our internal bank account of love. It is the bottom line. It is the deciding factor as to whether we engage our wings for high radiant and vibrational living, or whether we hide, cower, and self-depreciate in the corners of our lives. Regardless of the fall, compassion says that there is always the next moment, where love is present and available yet again for our deeper awareness. In this practice of self-compassion, you will find less destruction, more joy; a shorter refractory period of time in the shadows; less effort, more ease; less fear, more love. This is compassion's power. This is living from your heart.

Kwan Yin, through Doreen Virtue's book, encourages each of us to "Be blank. Be open. And know that whatever comes to you is good, and a lesson in the making." It is with the utmost gentleness that the lotus petals of your heart open. Be kind and loving to yourself and see what happens, feel your heart relax, and awaken in love.

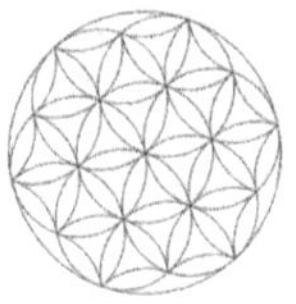

Shangri-Love 100 Percent Acceptance Activities:

BEING WITH THE PRESENT MOMENT PRACTICE

Just for the moment, just for the hour, just for the day, practice the art of saying okay. It is much easier to change when we have let go of our judgments and are free to maneuver again, to slowly take steps in a different direction. Simply allow yourself to BE more this week. Allow yourself to be aware that you don't have the whole picture yet. Accept that you are a vast being, complex, many faceted; that there are many different aspects of yourself that you don't even know yet. Consider that nothing happens that is not sanctioned by Spirit. If it has happened, it has happened. Practice being with the present moment.

REMOVING HEART RESIDUE BREATHING PRACTICE

If at any point you begin to feel blocked or stuck in negativity, stop and take a break to remove the heart residue. Try this three-minute meditation from Kundalini yoga. It is a fantastic way to hit your reset button if you find yourself stressed and all tied up in a knot during the day.

• Find a place to pause and relax for three minutes

• Sit up straight with your neck and back upright.

• Take a deep breath in and release it.

• Now, breathe in to the count of four, and breathe out to the count of one. Set a timer for three minutes. Continue breathing in to the count of four and breathing out to the count of one. At the end of the three minutes, take a deep breath in and hold it while rolling your shoulders forward. Hold for ten seconds and release, relaxing all the muscles in your shoulders and neck. Repeat the shoulder roll one more time by breathing in deeply, rolling your shoulders forward, holding your breath for ten seconds, and releasing your breath and shoulders to relax back to resting position.

Visualize letting go of all thoughts, grievances, or whatever emotions are challenging you at the moment at the start of this breathing practice; then picture it all being released as you complete it. Repeat as often as you would like throughout the day.

CHAPTER 8:

THE ULTIMATE MIRROR

*The end of all flight is to land. And when we land, we don't
lose our access to Heaven. We enter it.*
~Mark Nepo

My wings were engaged, I was spending time in stillness
and solitude and practicing self-compassion more and
more. I felt different. I felt lighter, more joyful. My
confidence was blooming. My ability to turn within to know
my own feelings and to recognize my patterns was growing.
And wouldn't you know that's when life sent in a test of my
inner strength—a true test of my ability. It's as if life was
testing to see if I could step beyond my attachment to
external circumstances, to see if I'd built the muscles to
navigate from my heart. And life sent this in the form of—

relationship. Now you might initially be asking, wait a minute, weren't you on a relationship sabbatical? Yep, I sure was. And out of the blue, right in the middle of my sabbatical, I got this message one day on the Internet from a guy who worked at my spiritual center. It read:

Zemirah~

*God, you are beautiful! I mean **so** beautiful! So radiant from the inside out that I get tongue-tied when I see you. I don't want to make you uncomfortable telling you this—I am just trying to call it out, so when I see you I don't feel like a high school boy with a crush—so I can just talk with you authentically. Maybe telling you this will make it worse, but hopefully I can just acknowledge it and release my inner awkwardness! So, feel free to just ignore this message if you want—I won't be offended. Peace, Zemirah. You carry a brilliantly bright light within! T*

It was one of those moments where the background music stopped playing and all was silent and frozen for a bit. There I was, immediately struggling with the old feisty and alluring pull of romance, my inner romantic already planning a candlelight dinner at sunset on a mountaintop nearby, *and* the unexpected words created a warm stir within me, which was followed by a wash of gratitude. I felt an instant reverence for my growth path. I mean, Wow!—wasn't this a change from some of the correspondence I'd been getting right before my sabbatical? I sat in this gratitude and allowed it to fill my heart. This was exactly the sort of communication that I was looking for in a relationship, exactly the stuff!

But then a cautious pause arrived. My deeper intention hit me square in the face. I considered my present experiences of Shangri-Love. I didn't immediately respond—in fact, I didn't respond at all for a couple of days. I sent some energetic gratitude that man's way, and sat down to be present with myself for a moment. While definitely intrigued, I sensed that it wasn't the time for distraction; it wasn't the time to get on that horse and ride off into the sunset. I sat with myself and allowed all the feelings to rise up. I sat in appreciation. And my resolve to continue building my relationship with me was deep. My dedication felt fierce. The energy of my sankalpa floated through me. So after my meditation, I simply sent him a message, thanking him for his generous, heartfelt sharing, honoring the light within him that was seeing the light within me and left it at that. However, the message from the Universe was not lost on me. I knew this note carried with it clues to the energy that I wanted to create in my life, so I wrote out his words and put them on the fridge. Although I had no desire to shift out of the yummy, heart-cave presence I was cultivating, I did want the Universe to know that this was exactly the kind of communication I eventually wanted to manifest—not with this man in particular, necessarily (although I felt his beautiful heart and loving spirit) but with someone, eventually. My message to God was: "This or something like it and thank you but not right now!" Months passed and I continued on my merry way, exploring more of the depths of Shangri-Love.

My Growth Vortex

Charles Albert Marks, who was quoted in Peter Kelder's *Ancient Secret of the Fountain of Youth, Book 2*, stated that, "Through the use of time-lapse photography, it has been shown that when a seed germinates, it does not shoot straight out of the ground, rather it spirals upward." This was the pattern of growth I experienced during this part of my life. As I strengthened my inner relationship with myself and began to expand my heart wings, life brought me the challenges necessary for me to polish my compassion, self-acceptance, and ultimate intention of cultivating a deep, loving connection to Spirit within myself. Just as the seed does not take a direct path in sprouting, but reaches and then appears to turn back toward the ground as it unfolds toward the light, my life was following a similar pattern of growth. I would reach toward the light, only to feel as if I spiraled backwards toward the dark.

There were some days where my inner mean girl still wanted to judge me incessantly. Sometimes I would encounter an unexpected bill, such as my car needed a repair or the dishwasher stopped working, making my finances teeter-totter and igniting my worry about being able to support myself and the girls. Those bumps in life still activated old feelings of being alone. There were times when I felt overwhelmed with responsibility and single parenting; it seemed like too much to handle. These moments were the times I felt like I took a step backwards, especially if my emotions took over for a while and threatened to derail my progress. Regardless, I kept showing up for the practice.

Life is a growth spiral. While I tend to expect a straight shot toward perfect balance, that belief is not actually based in reality and sets me up to feel bad when my life appears to detour. This was the case as Spirit delivered a life-changing relationship to me. I was experiencing more and more love and feelings of well-being, but it's as if life had a plan to take this growth deeper. It was in this precise moment that I received a grand mirror of relationship, one that showed me more of what was in my heart, both the light and the dark that was just waiting to be drawn into greater awareness.

Reflection of the Heart:
The Mirror of Relationship

It all started with a parent/child "playdate." Remember the man who sent me the beautiful message many months ago? Well, he happened to post something on Facebook about consciousness. I posted a comment, and soon we were meeting to hang out as single parents with kids. We both agreed that a dating relationship wasn't the idea of these meetings. But, have you ever tried to hold back the ocean? That was what it was like. After a couple of weeks, we were fully drawn in by the unavoidable pull of love. We read all the same books! We attended the same spiritual center—well, he worked there—and we had conversations about important, captivating stuff, like consciousness and holographic universes. This man, Todd, even owned the same astrology book I'd used during my dating days to determine compatibility! That, to me, was a huge sign that something grander in collaboration was afoot. Feeling our mutual attraction, we consulted the stars through this book. It essentially said, "Want to know more about self-love? Want someone who mirrors back to you the places that need love? Then this is the partner for you."

According to the book, we shared the exact same astrological birth number. No, we don't share a birthday, but we sure did share this particular life-lesson astrological make-up. I realize that may initially sound so romantic and "soul mate-like," and it was, initially. We were perfectly matched in many interests and passions. We traveled, hiked in nature, colored mandalas, cooked delicious meals, read poems in bed, wrote love notes, believed in the value of Epsom salt baths and vitamin supplements, loved our kids and parenting, and went to church together (something I had always deeply valued in a relationship). And his son and my daughter quickly became the best of friends.

All this felt wonderful but there was one other thing—our basic relationship fears and other related fears were also perfectly matched. This would prove to be monumentally challenging.

True soul mates, I believe, aren't the people who share favorite colors, eat the same foods, or have the same dreams. Nope, these are the souls who bring forth the greatest growth opportunities. They are the souls who mirror our darkest hurts, the ones whom love has not soothed. These interactions typically aren't gentle, smooth, or quiet, but rather are the monumental earthquakes of relationship that upend our internal circuitry and prompt us to expand our spiritual selves. Todd's and my relationship was one such connection!

John Goldthwait, PhD, in his book *Purifying the Heart*, writes about this "partners as mirrors" phenomenon. He states,

> "Couples are often attracted to each other
> because their inner relationships with them-
> selves are similar. Your partner's ways of
> being loving and unloving will usually re-
> flect your own, giving the relationship a feel-

ing of familiarity and even comfort. The degree of unlovingness will be about the same,
although it may occur in different areas so
may not be apparent."

After the initial love bubble phase of our relationship, Todd and I began a deeper calling. I was finally going to build my ability to experience Shangri-Love in the midst of relationship, but not without diving deeper into the parts of me that weren't awakened to love.

Early on in our relationship, my beloved Todd gave me a picture—one that resonated with me so much that I put it in my office, where it sits to this day. It's an image of a ferocious scaly dragon, open-mouthed, with a delicate fairy perched on its outstretched, clawed hand. The fairy is leaning over with a slight smile, arms crossed on the dragon's nose, looking pleasantly into the yellow, fierce, glowing eyes. We often discussed this photo. To us it symbolized the hero's journey we were on. We had found each other and the charge was to become an adult in relationship. If we could summon the fairy to mindfully meet the inner dragons of fear, then we would triumph in experiencing more love.

I felt determined to learn to love myself at the essence level of my soul so that I could love and accept my partner in the same way. If I could find a way to build the muscles, so to speak, to look beyond our behaviors and to genuinely honor our hearts, then I would finally find the nature of unconditional love. This would enable me to experience it more within and also deepen my ability to share it with others. But first, there would be a period of drawing up and out all the "inner dragons of fear."

GETTING SQUEEZED

Over the years I heard the teacher Wayne Dyer say many times, "If you squeeze an orange, out comes orange juice. What will come out if we squeeze you?" And then he would go on to explain that if there is anger inside, when squeezed, out will come anger. If there is compassion and love inside, then, when squeezed, out will come compassion and love. Our relationship was the ultimate juicer in my life. I mean, all the relationships in my life have been juicers of some sort or another, but this one was the Ultimate Omega Juicer 1000 model, both centrifugal and masticating, spinning me right into all that was inside and giving me a choice as to what I wanted to spit out and leave behind. It provided the ultimate opportunity to see what was inside me.

When I was squeezed, my default pattern had been to collapse into my emotions, whether it was sadness or anger or some of both. I had the tendency to cry or to lash out in anger during an argument. Not only that, but when I was really, *really* squeezed, I would withdraw and begin to hold back from connection with my partner. What did this look like? In the past, it looked like running away or breaking up. I believe I generally have a high tolerance for squeezing or conflict in relationship, but over time I would slowly pull away and close my heart until eventually only a wall remained. That is when I would slam the door and the relationship would be completely finished. Remember the dating in Neverland? Well, during that period, a couple of my relationships looked like a light switch being turned on and off and on and off. Furthermore, when squeezed, instead of rolling up my sleeves to tend to my heart, I often would set about trying to fix the world around me, and that often involved my focusing on my partner and what was "wrong" with him. All this fixing and my various avoiding behaviors were the armor that I used to not face pain or conflict in relationship. I desperately wanted love, safety, and security as everyone does, but I was still subtly looking for it in relationship with others rather than with myself. How easy it was to forget!

This relationship with Todd was my ultimate practice field. I now had the biggest challenge, one in which I could step beyond the old behaviors and patterns into a new way of loving. I knew this intellectually, but putting it into practice was incredibly difficult. Just like when flower buds that are forced to open, die, the more I pushed and prodded in Todd's business, business that wasn't mine to attend to, the more our relationship suffered lethal blows.

I knew I was doing it, but in my own fear and pain, I couldn't seem to get a handle on my patterns. I so deeply wanted to cultivate what Stephen Levine and Ondrea Levine refer to in *Embracing the Beloved,*

> "Mother Teresa, when asked how she could work in the midst of so much difficulty, said that she saw her ill and dying patients only as 'Jesus in his distressing disguise.' So looking across the breakfast table at another working on the edge of their pain, working to heal a lifetime's confusion and dismay, we slowly see the problem of relationship, the pain we all carry, and begin to recognize our partner in times of such confusion and dismay simply as 'the Beloved in its distressing disguise.'"

This was the invitation from love: could I learn to maintain focus on myself in the midst of another?

I entered into a period of relationship where I began to do some shadow work to expand compassion for others and myself. It reminded me of a story I'd heard several years earlier from a spiritual teacher who presented at my church. During the talk he spoke about an experience he had at the airport where he encountered a grumpy Transportation Security Administration (TSA) agent. He found the person's behavior rude. He shared how his initial thought about the rudeness was to judge that person, but then he stopped and asked himself where that behavior could potentially exist within him. He struggled at first because he didn't feel as if he was a particularly rude person, but then he looked deeper and embraced the capacity within himself to be rude. That's where he found compassion, when he embraced that he *could* be rude. This stuck with me over the years. Again and again I would return to that story in my mind. I identified with that teacher in that I sometimes couldn't initially find the behavior I am judging. For example, overall, I don't find myself to be particularly rude. However, I do see that the capacity to be rude does exist in me and there have been some times in my life where I was rude. What if those were the clues? What if Spirit was sending me hints as to where I hadn't embraced the shadow side of myself? What if the behaviors I was resisting in my beloved partner, Todd, were in fact mirroring back to me a deeper part of myself that I was not aware of, had not owned or embraced?

These questions really supported me during this time. Every time we began to spiral into our pattern of conflict, I would ask this golden question, "Where does that behavior or quality that I am resisting in him exist or live within me?" And, know what? Soon, in the quietness, I began to actually awaken to the places within me where the pattern I was resisting in Todd's behavior actually existed within me. Sometimes it hadn't surfaced yet, but certain thoughts or inclinations represented the potential. In this way I returned the focus to my growth and began to use our relationship and our challenges as catalysts for a deeper understanding of my own behaviors and myself in relationship to others. I was beginning to expand my ability to see a bigger picture of life.

COMMUNICATING THE TOUGH STUFF

One night Todd and I went out to dinner, just the two of us, and had a wonderful time. We talked and joked and laughed— we were really enjoying each other. It began to take a turn for the worse, however, when we got in the car to head home. Todd was learning to share his pain and I was learning how to listen without fixing anything. We were trying to find a conscious way to the middle ground. This night I was experimenting with a new way of interaction in an effort to break my old pattern (an illusion) of "fixing" my partner and was attempting to stay focused on myself. I wanted simply to witness his beautiful heart as he was trying to get me to feel his pain. This was a huge challenge for me, however—the tension grew as I sat there, squirming inside. I said little and attempted to be present. Todd could sense my discomfort. As the cycle continued, Todd's frustration was growing at my muted response and I eventually disintegrated into a hot mess.

I had learned growing up that "helping" was "loving," not realizing that it assumed that something was "wrong."

It was so difficult!! I could feel the volcano gathering force within me. I felt that if I even opened my mouth, I would spew a torrent of "spiritual" principles or quotes from the latest book I'd read to try and move him to a place that felt more comfortable to ME. I'd also learned growing up that avoiding intense or negative emotion was "nicer." I didn't want to see his pain nor share it, and the fact that he was trying to share it with me scared the heck out of me.

The more I contemplated our difficulties in communication, the more I saw the image of three circles. Two complete circles on each side of the equation interconnecting to form one central circle in the middle. The ones on each side represented each of us individually, each taking care of ourselves. And then I saw our sacred relationship as the interconnected circle in the center. This was the space where we went to dance together and to love. I saw how important it was that the center circle be used only for sacred nurturing of the relationship itself. Because it was just developing its own sacred identity, it felt to me that we should treat it with delicate touch, sacred reverence. It wasn't strong yet, nor created with the intention to define us, or to heal us. Nor was it designed to "support" us emotionally or physically, as it was in creation phase. Once our own circles were solidly healthy and the old patterns of codependency released, perhaps we would seek to define our relationship circle differently. But our charge for the moment was to continue to strengthen our awareness of Shangri-Love within.

There was an invitation on the table. Did we both want to create a sacred circle of relationship? Could we each share what we wanted and listen to each other? Did we both want to strengthen our own individual circles and commit to practicing authentic communication and listening throughout the process? What ingredients were essential for our sacred circle of relationship? Would we try to let go of behaviors that weren't loving or honoring of each other? Could we agree on what those were?

A few short months later, we had reached the point of decision. Our shadows had essentially taken over and I was having trouble seeing the forest for the trees, so to speak. I couldn't get a handle on the present and old patterns were spinning around me like a mobile. The pain inside me was reaching critical mass, a real hurricane of emotions. It was in this eye of the storm that I read Marianne Williamson's book *Enchanted Love,* in which she states,

> "If God comes first in our lives, then we are clear from whence we derive our sustenance. God is the only partner we *need.* The human at our side is a partner we *desire.* A clear difference between the two puts our inner world in balance, and then, and only then, can love rule all things."

Once again, I prayed for the transformation of love in my life. I was ready to let go completely, submitting my whole heart to God.

Then, during a coaching session, one of my coaches mentioned that she was going on a trip to Abadiânia, Brazil, to visit the Brazilian healer João Teixeira de Faria, known as John of God. I had heard about John of God before, as I'd seen on an episode of *Dateline NBC* and read about him through Gabrielle Bernstein, Wayne Dyer, and Oprah's experiences, but it was still way down on my bucket list. John of God is a healer and medium who allows "spirit doctors" to take over his body as he performs healings. Thousands of people visit from around the world each year to experience the loving energy of his spiritual hospital, known as the Casa. He'd built this healing center in a small rural town in central Brazil. When my coach mentioned this trip, I felt an immediate "yes" inside of me. I consulted with Todd and he fully supported the idea. Within seventy-two hours the rest of my world had rearranged to accommodate this voyage, including my daughters being invited on a two-week vacation with their father, which coincided perfectly with my pilgrimage dates! I followed my heart and signed up. I believed that the power of John of God and the entities that worked within him could, once and for, all shift my old patterns and truly set me free into unconditional love. The particular patterns of codependence that I was considering were the roots of my old dating escapades and, I sensed, the roots of my present relationship challenges: reliance on my partner to "make me happy," my tendency to get into other's business to "fix" things, and my feelings of being completely abandoned in single parenthood. All of these little sticky monsters were the culprits that kept me from the deeper experience of connection and Shangri-Love in the midst of relationship, with both others and myself.

As I went about preparing for the trip, part of Krishna Das' song, "Sri Argala Stotram," reverberated in my head. It was the part where he included lyrics from the band Foreigner: "I want to know what love is, and I want You to show me." I wholeheartedly sang this prayer over and over again. I felt like I had the soul stamina and was ready to be rid of these monsters once and for all. I was ready to know unconditional love. I meditated on my intentions during the weeks leading up to my journey.

I Want to Know What Love IS

Arriving in Abadiânia, I could feel an energetic change, a sort of weight to the energy, not heavy, but deeper. At the risk of sounding cliché, I felt anchored in love. I felt anchored in nature, as if it were breathing and expanding through me instead of around me. I was a part of the world, but I also sensed being a part of something much, much greater, as if many worlds were accessible all at once.

I thought about how I wanted to continue deepening in relationship with Todd, but not at the expense of our individual health and balances. I was open to whatever needed to happen on this journey to realize my deepest intentions of healing. The first night I picked up my phone to text and was just about to engage in an age-old pattern of emotionally asking for attention in a less than balanced way, and the door to my posada room began to rattle furiously as if someone was trying to come in. I dropped the phone. I clearly heard in my mind, *Stop, put that phone down!* I dropped it like it was a hot potato and didn't pick it up again until morning, when I deleted the mid-sentence message I'd been typing. *Send only love,* was the message in my head, and I was blessed with an instant knowing that Spirit had intervened even before I'd made my first visit to the Casa. That was the end of my drama-seeking behaviors and has been since. They were more or less unconscious, but in that moment I was blessed that they entered the realm of my consciousness and I immediately stopped.

My first steps on the Casa property were accompanied with feelings of slight nausea and a brief dizziness. I felt a bit disoriented. I shared this with our trip guides and set the intention for Spirit to build my internal circuitry so that I may be of greater service in the world. The first morning session, we walked into a huge room filled with chairs with a stage at the far end. There were pictures of various saints and healers on the wall, such as John the Baptist and the Dalai Lama. There was a large wooden triangle securely fastened to the wall of the stage where people could place their prayers. The room was filled to the brim with people. As we walked in and sat in the front, my heart began to beat wildly in my chest. I breathed. I grounded the energy moving through me. After a few moments, I motioned to our trip leader that I was moving to the back of the room. It felt to me that the farther I was from the stage, which was presently empty, the less strong the energy would be, kind of like being away from an epicenter of energy. I sat back there and continued to ground myself and to breathe.

The next morning, I headed to a spot called the Overlook after breakfast. It was a wooden balcony built to overlook the dense Brazilian rainforest valley below. I sat alone in silence, feeling the gentle breeze on my skin. It was like all time was at a still point, the entire world held in the peacefulness of this place. I felt rooted in love as I sat on the beautiful, varnished, wooden benches, as if actual roots were growing from within me and connecting to the earth and sky. It became a ritual of mine to get up early, scarf down some breakfast as fast as possible and race down to the Overlook to sit and be present in the morning air. As I sat there my mind would gradually settle into calmness and I could feel the current of love flow within me (it's not that it was never not flowing, it's just that my awareness settled so that I could genuinely track its presence within me). I felt rooted in love and well-being and had no impulse to break the flow of energy I felt while sitting there.

As I watched each day, eventually a flock of blackbirds would begin to circle in the air above. One day, as they circled around, I gazed at them and became mesmerized. I felt their ease and grace of flight. It was as if I hadn't ever seen a bird before! I took videos of their flight on my phone, and, arriving home I giggled, since I could barely see anything on what I captured. Time seemed to fall away and there were only the birds and the trees before me. I felt complete peace on the planet. Sometime tears of gratitude would just flow down my cheeks. It seemed like this emotion just spontaneously appeared. Once expressed, it would flow through and stop as suddenly as it had emerged. I was in this cloud of allowing everything to be just as it was. Such peacefulness.

While I was at the Casa and around the grounds, I witnessed miracles. Not only the miracles associated with John of God, but miracles of love. People from different cultures speaking different languages were united and singing songs; many languages intermingled with grace. It was a tapestry of love. I saw no distinction or lines of culture drawn to separate one from the other.

There were so many instances of helping others. I saw people offering seats to those who needed to sit down in the heat. I saw strangers fanning each other. I saw people helping others who struggled to walk, gain balance from a supporting hand. I saw one woman in a wheelchair, who was a beaming light and joy to everyone she met, have a different person each day pushing her across town, accompanying her home. She would instantly bond with people and extend welcoming energy and love. Another day, I bonded in the line with a woman from Spain. Since I'd studied and lived in Spain, we conversed in Spanish. When she learned I was a school psychologist, she asked for my help for her grandson in Turkey who was struggling in school. After I gave her some ideas about how she might support him in relaxing and increasing his attention span, she asked for my business card for the kidsrelaxation.com website and said, "You never know, maybe someday you will come and teach the children in Turkey." My heart was wide open, feeling the beautiful connections that Spirit was orchestrating simply by virtue of all of us united in this powerful energy, seeking healings.

When I finally went before John of God, I was initially dismissed to get herbs and a crystal-bed session. However, on return and holding current (meditating) for an entire day, I was instructed to have my first spiritual intervention. I wholeheartedly gave myself to the process. I felt the intensity of my commitment within myself as I asked for support with my emotional body and physical body. That night I felt as if I could not even speak, as if I'd had a one million times strength Reiki treatment. I slept for sixteen hours. All the while, I never felt afraid. Quite the opposite, I felt this blanket of love all around me. I would hear things in my mind as I was sleeping such as, *all is okay, you are being restored,* or once, I felt an instruction to turn over. There were pains throughout my body. When I woke up I felt a hundred times lighter, as if a weight had been removed from my neck and back. The energy over the following days came in waves.

There were moments when I felt so vibrant and alive and others when I needed to rest and lie down.

One night I wrote out four pages of memories, resentments, and grievances toward others and myself—all the things I wanted to release. I focused on all the relationships throughout my life to this point, every grievance I held against others and every grievance I held against myself. Then I completed a prayer and began to cry as I said the words of release, and felt a deep knowing that it was completed. A wave of knowing that I was genuinely stepping beyond old energetic patterns passed over me.

The next day brought a visit to the sacred waterfall, deep in the forest beneath the Overlook. Again, as we descended the path through the trees to the waterfall, I felt the energy surge around me like a heaviness, not in oppression, but in intensity. When we reached the waterfall and I dipped my head in the breathtakingly cold waters, I knew all was completely released and let go. Stepping up to wade, I looked up to see a huge dragonfly appear overhead and hover for a moment before flying away. To me, it symbolized my rebirth and transmutation of old energy into new, the shift from fear to love. Walking back up the path after my waterfall baptism, I felt more tears of gratitude and release, sobbing away, not with sadness but with freedom and peace.

A few days later, I returned to visit John of God and the entity instructed me to sit in the entity chairs directly to the side of John of God. I knelt before the entity, and he, in good humor, began to talk with me and invited me to "hold current" in one of the entity chairs lining the wall directly in front of him. Sitting down, I felt the intense energy of the five-plus foot crystals nearby and all the energy of the entities working through John of God as well as the hundreds of other meditators holding current in the room. It was as if deep meditation was instantaneous and the world went dark. I entered a blankness of pure love and the deep energy of Presence. Three hours passed like ten minutes. I didn't have visions or really any thought at all for all that time, just the experience of a heavy, peaceful, rather blank "nothingness" of well-being.

Afterwards my whole body was shaking and I quickly walked back to my posada and collapsed into tears of release. I'm not sure what I was releasing, exactly, but I just cried and cried until I felt complete. I still had no thoughts other than gratitude and a feeling of integration within myself, as if all my pieces and thoughts and feelings were simply aligning within.

The next morning, I was instructed to sit in the entity chairs again, to the side of John of God. The energy I felt was similar to what I'd experienced the day before, however, this time I did have some visions. As I sat there, my shoulder began to throb with pain. I breathed and witnessed the pain, allowing and welcoming it, as it signified for me that the beings of light were working within it. As the ebb and flow of pain surged, a series of past memories of various relationship conflicts and even childhood memories of conflict flooded my mind. I looked on with interest, suddenly realizing that the beings of light were showing me directly what I must release in order to completely heal. It was a meditation of self-empowerment. I felt intense gratitude. I meditated and felt the unwinding of stuck energy begin to seep out of my body and flow away.

Then I started to receive creative ideas. I thought of things that would support children in relaxation. I thought of people with whom I'd had conflicts. I imagined my ex-mother-in-law and ex-husband in the light. During this five-plus hour meditation, I had this glimpse of all people as love, this awareness and "big picture" view of every single moment of my life as it had conspired for me to more greatly know love, feel love, and understand that God and ALL is love. I sensed how every person is on an individualized path to experience love at the deepest level and that there are just myriad strange ways and behaviors that people adopt to achieve a deeper understanding of love. I felt like compassion was being born in a more genuine way within me. For me, it was the answer to my prayer. A huge revelation! As this compassion flooded through me I began to gently send light out into the room; as if it were emanating from within me. A heartbeat of light and love was pulsing into the room from my heart. I saw the room filled with light. There were hundreds of people passing through the line before me and although my eyes were closed, I also sensed them being bathed in this light.

After nearly two weeks, my visit to John of God came to an end. As I was on the long flights back to Denver, I reflected on my journey. I set an intention for myself. I thought about the simplicity of the life down in Abadiânia and how wonderful it felt to be immersed in this simple way of being. For me it was Shangri-Love expressed. Life can be slow, mindful, and centered in love. I vowed to keep my daily practice of "holding current" in meditation and being in the current to maintain and further deepen my awareness of love.

The energy shifts in my house and relationship were profound as a result of this journey of awakening. For example, I shifted the way we made dinner, establishing a family ritual of "cooking with love" or "CWL" so that we could all engage in the process of infusing love into our food while connecting with one another at the same time. Todd experienced many shifts as a result of the trip as well. He had given me a picture of himself to take down to be blessed by John of God and was prescribed herbs as a result. When I took his picture in front of John of God, the entity said he was going to personally conduct healing work with Todd that evening. Todd and I were finally, for the moment, able to answer the questions that had been raised before my trip. Yes, we were willing to grow deeper. Yes, we wanted to develop the sacred relationship and continue to work on our sacred relationships with ourselves. Our prayer time, while established before, now became rock solid. The grace of God was at work in our life . . . and BIG TIME.

What I found at John of God was not a complete Pollyanna swipe to my life, but rather the spiritual traction necessary to address the patterns that I took down there. I now had more traction to align more with my spirit and less with my ego and to achieve what Stephen Levine and Ondrea Levine were referring to as being able to see past pain to the beloved in myself, my children, and in Todd. It's not that Todd and I haven't experienced triggers since, but this traction gave me the ability to disengage from my emotions enough to move into response rather than reactivity. I no longer felt ruled by my emotions. I now felt as if my heart had a say as to how I respond to my life. I had more power to activate compassion when my behaviors and the behaviors of others were not loving. I got clear on my boundaries and my definition of what was loving and respectful. I made a non-negotiable pact with myself to take a break when I feel off-center. I made a commitment to give others space when they request it or conflict is escalating. It also has become easier for me to share my feelings with grace. In this way, respect and love have taken root in my relationships with my loved ones, and I have become more fully responsible for all my interactions.

THE BAROMETER OF LOVE

The journey to deepen in love is ongoing. It's easy to have a "spiritual experience" and to feel all healed and lighter and wonderful, but to quickly forget that it is a continuing process of spiritual practice, growth, and development. I shared my John of God experience to relay the greater unfolding of love in my life, but it certainly is not the only way to have that experience! I realize that not everyone feels called to journey to Brazil; it may not be your path. The main point is that I dove into an experience that enabled me to connect with myself more than I had before. There are an infinite number of ways for anyone to do that.

After the John of God experience, I began to implement a new sort of barometer in my life, one that I totally love. It is the "Is this love?" barometer. In the presence of any situation, I go within to feel the pulse point of love. In this way, the pulse point directs my response to life. This is my heart. This is my love. This is living my love story with me. This is the barometer I continue to use and that continues to take me deeper into Shangri-Love. Looking back, it seems that when I truly decided to start honoring myself in relationship with other, but most important in relationship to myself, that Spirit began to organize around *that*. And, honor in relationship began to truly show up in my experience.

CHAPTER 9:

LIVING SHANGRI-LOVE

The heart is a thousand-string instrument
that can only be tuned with love.
~Hafiz

When I was a little girl, my sister and I would join my grandmother and great-grandmother at dusk to watch moonflowers open. Thirty minutes before the sun was scheduled to sink below the horizon, we would gather the lawn chairs on the back lawn, amid the strawberries, peonies, and irises, and wait. Sometimes a train would thunder by on the tracks that ran through the tiny Midwest town. The pace of life was slow, the essence of the moment was felt, and the magic in my heart was alive as I watched the gradual, delicate un-spiraling of those long, white

trumpets. How gracefully the flowers unfolded, each reaching a final instant where all the petals were freely open, ready to bask all night in the moonlight.

Those moonflowers are like my journey into living connected to my Shangri-Love. Just as the tightly coiled flower buds opened to the sweet gentleness of the moonlight, opening my heart has been a slow spiral of letting go of judgments and relaxing into acceptance; acceptance of others, of myself, and of life as it is. It has been a process of becoming fully present within my heart, an ongoing process that never ends. As a result, a sort of integration has begun to take place. In the letting go of old energy in the form of grievances toward myself and others, releasing limiting beliefs from my subconscious, and connecting with my heart in stillness, I have discovered the part of myself that is whole, complete, and perfect just the way it is. When my energy was previously tied up in all that noise, I was fragmented;

my attention was pulled in many directions, most of which were in the past or future. By spending time in my heart, I am in the present now and that deep place within my heart, which I refer to as Shangri-Love, is changeless. It is a drop of Spirit that is eternal, a pool of unconditional love.

So what does living in Shangri-Love look like? How do you access this place again and again to be present with your heart? It looks like staying open to life as it is in any given moment, allowing it to flow rather than getting stuck in resistance. It looks like trusting that Spirit is the chief architect of life, so you can relax now. It looks like trusting that in life, all paths lead to the center and Spirit is conspiring to lead you into deeper awareness of your true essence, your Shangri-Love. It is about realizing that there is no destination, and nothing to "fix." There's only a deeper drawing out of the inherent love within you and your natural state of being. How do you experience all this? You allow life to be as it is and are fully present, releasing the attachment to needing to figure things out.

OPEN OR CONTRACTED?

What Shangri-Love doesn't look like is a constant state of happiness, but rather is a state of centeredness. It's not about being happy all the time; rather it's a matter of navigating the ups and downs of life while practicing the return to center. With Shangri-Love, I deepen my ability to stay open during the ebb and flow, off and on, light and dark of life. Sometimes I feel more connected to Spirit, sometimes less (although I am always connected, we all are always connected). Sometimes things are flowing like a well-oiled machine and sometimes it seems like the emergency brake is on. But what I've learned is that the more my heart stays open in the midst of the bumps and dark alleys of life, the less residue builds up—the stuff that keeps me from accessing the deeper beauty of my life. The trick is building my capacity to stay open as opposed to shrinking down in self-protection or retreating into my mind.

The more I spend time in my heart, awakening my heart, the more I allow life's ebbs and flows to happen, (the more I navigate from a place of centeredness, a balanced middle ground). It's what I think Buddha was referring to when he spoke about "the middle way, the way between all extremes." I've come to refer to this place as living from a place of "and." "AND" has been my integration point. When something in my life goes crazy for a moment, I remember that light AND dark exist in a dynamic universe. See, I used to jump squarely into black and white thinking. When things were going well, my life was a total rose. When things would go bump, my psyche would take a nosedive into catastrophic thinking; I was sure that the apocalypse was now. My strategy while living in Shangri-Love is to remind myself that life is dynamic and constantly changing. Spending time in my heart has rooted me in acceptance. Now when things go upside-down, I remind myself that it's not a huge deal and breathe into accepting things the way they are. Being wholehearted, I activate the grace in my life to be with whatever IS in any given moment. Letting go of my attachments sets me free.

Since I've been exploring my Shangri-Love, I'm able to let go of the little stuff more easily. I'm able to let go when I get cut off in traffic or encounter a salesperson who is having a "bad" day. I'm able to let go when I drop my new iPhone on the concrete *again*, causing the glass screen to shatter. And not only am I able to more easily let go, but I can sometimes find the humor in my triggers and take myself more lightly.

I was triggered one day when my partner Todd and I had a misunderstanding. It started on a Saturday morning when he casually said he was making a cup for me as I headed downstairs to work in my office. You see, Todd makes the world's best cup of coffee—he is an expert. Every day he grinds the beans and carefully packs the grounds into the espresso machine. It is an art form. I am so blessed to have a specially prepared fresh ground cup of this "love" nearly every day of the year.

It turned out that this was one of those occasions where he meant one thing and I heard another. Thinking that he intended to deliver the coffee, I decided to surprise him with a beautiful ambiance. I lit candles, turned on some music, arranged a seating area for us to chat and anxiously awaited his arrival. After twenty minutes or so, I was still waiting, candles blazing. I went up and found my cup of coffee cooling by the espresso machine, with no Todd in sight. He'd gone out for a walk with the dogs! A little trigger went off inside. I felt indignation and disappointment. I mean, I had lit candles! He, of course, didn't know that. He'd made the coffee just like he said he would and carried on with his day. In a cloud of irritation, I went to track him down and share my disappointment. In the middle of my sentence, however, as I registered his surprised face, I began to laugh at the absurdity of it all. The more I spend time in my Shangri-Love, the easier it is for me to let go of insignificant triggers such as this. I mean it truly wasn't a big deal that my office surprise hit a dead end. Connecting within my heart often brings more lightheartedness to my life.

RELAX, SPIRIT'S GOT THIS

So how can you fully relax into the happenings of life? For me, it has been about realizing that I am not in charge of the world's spin on its axis. I remember once in the early days of my dating in Neverland, I attended a meditative gathering in the backwoods of Colorado. It took place at a cabin nestled by a roaring mountain creek. We had a private stone hot springs "pool" fed with hot mineral water pumped from deep in the earth. After an hour of prayer, dance, and singing, we each took turns being fully suspended beneath the stars. When it was my turn, I was held by the group, lifted up out of the water to lie beneath the "canopy of the heavens." Far from any neighboring town or other light pollution, the night sky was completely illuminated, a glorious display of the Milky Way and all the constellations. Lying there, completely relaxed and surrendered to the present moment, I could deeply connect with the sense that Spirit's got this. My realization in that moment was that I did not create the heavens (I know that seems obvious, but with the level of stress I felt during that period of my life, I'd been acting as if I was, in fact, responsible for creating the universe). I also had the thought that any being responsible for the infinite creation above and around me certainly could handle the concerns—no matter how large or small—of my life. It was quite an awakening on my part. To genuinely let go and let God be the director of my life's orchestra was such an incredibly freeing sensation: freeing my mind, my body, and my pent-up stressful emotions.

This realization was and is, of course, a continual process. My dear, long-time friend, Jen Walsh, is the best at delivering this reminder over and over. I will call her in a tizzy about something, seriously convinced that it's a big deal, and she will respond by saying, "God's got this." Immediately my worries will crumble to dust and the stress melts away when I hear those words.

Jen's reminder often helps to center me, but truly nothing drums the concept that Spirit's ultimately in charge into my awareness better than venturing into foreign lands. And, often, Spirit will remind me in the most exquisitely beautiful ways. A couple of years ago, Todd and I were vacationing and exploring Glastonbury, England, on a whirlwind tour that also included Iceland, France, and Ireland. We were staying in an incredible home, an Airbnb owned by the Glastonbury town architect, situated at the base of the Tor! When I booked the place, I had no idea what treasure awaited us.

It was the middle of the night and I suddenly awoke from a deep sleep. With my eyes closed, it seemed as if someone had switched on the overhead light in the room. But I opened my eyes to darkness, and Todd was still sleeping soundly at my side. The light of the full Moon was shining faintly through the wispy white curtains, but there was no light on in the room. I had a sudden, insistent thought. Clear as a bell I heard the words, "get up and go outside!" It was freezing at four in the morning, but I opened the French doors and tiptoed barefoot out onto the sprawling wooden patio overlooking the Somerset Levels, or "the summer country" where Glastonbury is located. There in front of me was an expansive vista of the terraced meadows in the marshy valley below; behind and above me the Tor reigned over it all.

My prayer on visiting Glastonbury was to see the "mists of Avalon." Having twenty years earlier read the notorious book of the same name, I had visions of dreamily dancing through the mist that connected the "otherworlds" from the day-to-day world that is known. Mist has always been a fascination of mine, as if it cloaks the world and allows dreams to be a little bit more tangible. I had even dreamed of the Tor prior to booking our room, somehow feeling compelled to visit. I often follow those heart urges, not knowing exactly what magic life has for me, but trusting that if I follow my heart, it will become clear. Glastonbury was no different. I felt some sort of magical enchantment with the place, and, walking the streets of the town felt a little like being dipped in the middle of a modern-day Renaissance Festival, complete with apothecaries, labyrinths, rose quartz crystals in shop windows, and an ancient pub, the George and Pilgrim Hotel, built in the 1400s and still in service today.

So, on that freezing predawn in the moonlight, I walked out and found the mists of Avalon transforming the valleys before me. I could see why Glastonbury was called Glastonbury, derived from the Welsh name, Ynis Witrin, meaning the Isle of Glass. It looked as if we were floating in the midst of a sea. I stood aghast; hardly daring to breathe for fear the scene might evaporate prematurely. It was indescribably beautiful.

The morning birds were just beginning their daily twitters, and what I felt, gazing out at those mists, was a deep gratitude and overwhelming sense that *Spirit's got this, I can relax now.*

What does this mean for your journey to Shangri-Love? What does it have to do with living in Shangri-Love? It means allowing life's contrasts to pull you deeper into acceptance rather than stimulate greater resistance within you. What if each moment of difficulty is actually, on a much deeper level, an expression of love? Living in Shangri-Love is not about denying the more difficult side of life, the challenging emotions or the resistance that pops up on the path. It's about learning to be present with these bumps in the road. And the next part of this journey is about trusting that regardless of the detours that appear to be happening in your life, you can trust that God is love. God is always conspiring to deepen your awareness of the Shangri-Love within you, should you choose to accept this challenge.

All Paths Lead to Center

Nothing demonstrates this concept better for me than the labyrinth. Labyrinths in present day, and most likely in ancient days as well, have been used as a meditative tool. A single, twisting, winding path that leads to a rose-petaled center, the labyrinth has a clear entry and a clear exit. Although the path winds around and around and often appears to be leading away from the center rather than toward, it eventually culminates at the center. There is one across town from my home that I visit regularly to clear my thoughts and get back to my center—my heart—especially when my thoughts are running rampant through my mind. When I walk a labyrinth, more often than not, I feel my thoughts settle and calm, like sand settling to the bottom of a jar of water.

I remember my first step onto the ancient labyrinth embedded in the floor of Chartres Cathedral in Chartres,

France. I immediately felt the energy of love, which brought instantaneous tears, not of sadness but simply a response to the love I felt churning up within me and rising to the surface. As my daughters and I walked the paths, tourists would wander in, oblivious to the labyrinth in the floor. They'd cut across it and stop, standing on it while looking up at the wondrous stained-glass windows above. They didn't seem to notice the pilgrims who were mindfully walking the path. Initially, I was irritated by their lack of awareness. But in looking at the labyrinth as a symbol for life as a whole, it wasn't lost on me the irony that often people or other "obstructions" cross or seem to even block my path. I contemplated how I am like that when I'm attuned to the outer world, staring up at the windows but forgetting to look for the deeper meaning, the one I could see if I just paused for a moment.

The labyrinth is a grand demonstration of the concept that "all paths lead to center." If we choose to accept the challenge, then every detour in life can be used to take us deeper into awareness. The obstructions can catalyze a deeper connection within our hearts, if we turn within, in the midst of the challenge.

Shangri-Love is always present within. All that's required is a turning within to access the love in the center of you. All of your life paths can lead to this center, this love, should you choose to simply observe the outer and turn within to the presence of Sprit in your heart. The Shangri-Love journey can be graceful and grace-filled if you remember to keep the big picture of life in perspective. Step back to view each path as a route to the center of your heart. It is like this quote from Marcel Proust: "The real voyage of discovery consists not in seeking new lands but seeing with new eyes." See your challenges with new eyes, and observe your emotions that arise as a result; be present with whatever is present. This presence connects you with your Shangri-Love.

FROM ERADICATING WEEDS TO FERTILIZING THE SOIL

I get that sometimes life can seem extremely overwhelming and the challenges can seem like too much. When I was in the midst of my dating frenzy, I often felt overwhelmed. I could sense that I was spinning my wheels in a land of eternal mud, but I wasn't sure how to shift out of the place I was in. The pain lying just below the surface felt scary and insurmountable, as if it were a can of worms that if opened, would result in a neverending cascade of discomfort. But eventually I reached a point where the pain was so great that I was propelled into taking action to shift it.

In the beginning I felt like I was playing "whack-a-mole" with the pain. Everywhere I looked, there was another "weed" to eradicate from the garden of my life. However, I also noticed that the more time I spent trying to get rid of the weeds, the less time I spent actually fertilizing the soil. Why am I sharing this now, in a chapter at the end of the book, in the chapter that is supposed to be about living within your heart? Because I believe living in the heart is about realizing that there's a part of us that's perfect, whole and complete, just as it is. This belief is what's helped me shift my thinking away from "something is wrong and I must fix or change it."

Fertilizing the soil through all of the methods I've shared—while not easy, perhaps—was far more aligned with love than my continued effort to "fix or change" things (which is actually an illusion and endless quest anyway). In recognizing our wholeness, we are freed from attachment to the conditions of life, and more at peace with "what is." At the level of the heart, all is whole, all is balanced, all is love; it's merely about drawing it out and expressing it.

♥

Becoming a gardener in my life means that I'm always focusing at the level of the soil and not at the level of the plant. My attention is on fertilizing the soil of my life by being fully present within me. This doesn't mean that there isn't an emotional release process through forgiveness, self-compassion, and other means. It means that my attention is on the brilliance of my heart and soul.

In my work with kids in the schools, I often remind parents and teachers that we are the gardeners, always planting seeds. As a gardener we are not responsible for when and if the seeds grow. This became super clear to me through my daughter's struggle with obsessive-compulsive disorder, as I introduced in Chapter Six. Even as a baby, Maiya showed food sensitivities and struggled to sleep. Although we got rid of gluten and experimented with various supplements, she continued to have anxiety, which eventually evolved into OCD. Stress amplified her symptoms, which often appeared as the need to tap things or repeat behaviors over and over. As a parent, I was terrified. I would wake up in the middle of the night filled with worry, looking for the next remedy to sample. As a school psychologist, I became distracted and fixated on the symptoms and set about trying to "fix" them.

But the more I tried to "figure things out," the more Maiya's symptoms seemed to stay the same, if not worsen. We tried all the usual therapy techniques, to no avail. Maiya would cry and struggle, wrestling with the monsters in her brain. Even with my arsenal of tools and techniques, I often felt paralyzed. It wasn't until one day as I dropped her off at grade school and watched helplessly as she tapped her lunchbox on the side-walk, dragging it all the way to the school doors, that I burst into tears. They were the tears of desperation and surrender. I was so scared and frustrated and angry at those symptoms, which seemed to steal my little girl's peace!

That was the first time I really got present with the thoughts and feelings floating around inside me. Instead of trusting Maiya's life path, I'd been trying to make the seeds grow! I was so focused on results that I forgot to be the gardener. My role was to plant the seeds; to offer tools or ideas to support and fertilize the soil with love. I couldn't *make* the plant grow. It had to do so on its own.

I heard a voice clearly in my mind say, *Look beyond this.* What if I took my focus off the symptoms and put my focus more on love? What if my greatest respect for her would be to accept and honor her path and the way she chose to meet it? I realized that while I could provide strategies for her that I be-lieved in, I needed to let go of my attachment to the outcome. My ultimate job as her mom was to love without conditions.

I continued to plant seeds and offer ideas, but I began to release my attachment to how she responded to the seeds. I wouldn't get so hung up on whether or not she listened to the guided meditation CD I left on her bed or read the books I suggested. I began to trust that her path was perfect for her. To do this, I had to let go, again and again.

As a parent, I believe it can be extremely difficult to deeply accept and trust that our children's paths may or may not be aligned with how we think they "should" be. It was hard for me to accept that Maiya might've needed her OCD journey for the purpose of an important soul development, one that I couldn't fully fathom.

After I let go, her symptoms didn't immediately disappear, but my attachment to their presence in her life decreased. Whether she was free of symptoms wasn't the point; what mattered was that we could find peace in the midst of the experience.

Maiya has a powerful will and dedication and she knows what works for her. She eventually found relief through running and by applying her brilliant mind in academic study, ultimately becoming valedictorian of her class. She found and engaged her heart wings again and again to meet OCD right where it was. In this, she has shown me another side to Shangri-Love. She couldn't take on all her thoughts or symptoms at once, but she could start with the thoughts she had in the moment and work from there. Her symptoms, while still present from time to time today, took a back seat to her dedication to doing her best, no matter what.

What I took away from Maiya's example was the importance of starting right where you are and getting present with that. So I invite you, in venturing out on your Shangri-Love journey, no matter the magnitude of struggle you may be facing, start where you are, take one small step toward love, and love will always be there to meet you. There is nothing to "fix." In the depth of your heart, all is whole and complete.

THE SIDE EFFECT IS INTEGRATION

So what happens if you begin to deeply trust that Spirit's got this, relaxing into your life bumps and all, and letting go of the emotional stuff inside? What happens if you begin to be more fully present within your heart? What if you begin to address the emotional residue within through forgiveness, acceptance, and self-compassion? What if you try meditations such as Neurosculpting and HeartMath and begin to rewrite your brain chemistry and activate your highest-order thinking ability and your heart center at the same time? What if you spend time in stillness and solitude, practice mindfulness, and take full responsibility for your life's creation? Integration is what happens, that's what! Through practicing all these concepts, your heart awakens. All the previous energy that was tied up in victimhood and old grievances will slowly be absorbed back into your heart, leaving only love.

With an awakened heart, more of you is present in the present moment. When you interact with others, you are fully connected to what is taking place instead of riding your triggering emotions off to another time in the past or the future. Instead of feeling that you or your circumstances are "less than," you have the sense that all is as it should be right now in the present moment.

VESICA PISCIS

I keep a symbol to remind me of my dedication to my Shangri-Love journey and the integration within my heart. It's called a vesica piscis, and it sits on my kitchen windowsill.

The vesica piscis is composed of two circles that interlock to create a fish symbol—an eye shape, of sorts—in the middle. It's a sacred geometry symbol that has been used throughout the centuries to stand for the union of spirit and matter. I first came in contact with it when I spied it on the ceiling of my spiritual center at Mile Hi Church in Lakewood, Colorado, directly in the center of our giant dome. I saw it again on our trip to Glastonbury, on the cover of the Chalice Well—two intertwining fish cast in wrought iron.

For me the vesica piscis represents the perfect integration found in the heart, the wholeness of our spiritual self. Living in Shangri-Love is the perfect intersection of your physical, emotional, thinking self with your spiritual, light-filled self; it is that place within you where all is unified and whole. My daughter, Maddie, drew this symbol for you. May it serve as a reminder to turn within again and again to access this place of love within you.

Creating a Vortex of Love

A vortex is a whirl of fluid or wind or any kind of mass. I envision it as a tornado-style circulation of energy. While I was visiting John of God, the image of vortex of love popped into my mind one day, as I was journaling. If I am responsible for creating my experience of the world, I reasoned, then I'd better be ultra-intentional about what I place within this "vortex of love." So I drew a "V" on a paper, thought about my barometer of love, and began to write and collect everything that I wanted to experience and express as love within the "V," including the following:

- respectful communication,

- deep listening,

- practicing being fully present with others, authentic and honest sharing,

- taking full responsibility for my actions and feelings,

- impeccable words,

- loving without conditions,

- expressions of gratitude,

- open-heartedness, and

- honoring the other as myself.

This wasn't about a shopping list for God; it was about more fully expressing the heart presence of Shangri-Love.

Michael Brown, in his book, *The Presence Process*, states, "Unconditional love must be given to be experienced, for it is through the act of giving that it is experienced." Along the way on this journey of Shangri-Love, I was looking to access love within myself and to share it, shifting away from "what can I get from the world" to "what can I give from the essence of love within me." So I began to place items within my vortex, knowing that I was creating a template for myself. If I got lost as the path unfolded, I would have the V to remind me of my intention.

You can create your own vortex of love by paying close attention to what you are selecting in your life. Are you transfixed with the junk food of too much social media? Are you hanging out with people who would rather gossip (another form of energetic junk food) rather than inspire? What do you fill your days with? Often these days, I believe, we are filling our time with impoverished data: negative news, fear-based trivia, and video games of instant gratification. Rather than carefully selecting the sort of information that is allowed into our bodies and minds, we allow the constant bombardment of a fast-paced society free rein. This non-mindful behavior is contributing, at least in my experience, to an attention-deficit/hyperactive disorder (ADHD) epidemic in our kids and within ourselves. The world is filled with fast-paced everything, from food, to games, to all other forms of entertainment. All this constant input deadens our ability to be present, to be still, and to deeply feel our own hearts.

I'm inviting you through these Shangri-Love concepts to connect with your heart, to make it your own barometer of love. When you are making a choice of what to read, what to watch, what to eat, or who to hang out with, ask yourself, "Does it resonate with love or does it resonate with fear?" Become ultra-mindful of what you are allowing into your body, mind, and heart. By spending time with your heart, you will hone your ability to discern.

Throughout this book I've shared the means through which I've become more present with myself, more present within my heart, how that place continues to evolve, and how I return to it again and again. It's a journey! Lao Tzu said it beautifully:

> "If you want to awaken all of humanity, then awaken all of yourself. If you want to eliminate the suffering in the world, then eliminate all that is dark and negative in yourself. Truly the greatest gift you have to give is that of your own self-transformation."

This alchemy of the heart, which I believe Lao Tzu is referring to, is about allowing love to transmute fear. It's about surrendering into the present moment and allowing life to be as it is. It's about awakening unconditional love by activating the transcendent observer and self-compassion. The result is integration within, the ability to navigate the duality of life and access peace at the same time.

The tools I've shared are some techniques that have worked for me but are by no means the only way. You are unique in what coaxes open the beautiful lotus of your heart—it is up to you to find what works.

Here is an invitation for you: bring the sacred back into your life. Look for ways to saturate your life with what you value the most, what you respect, what you revere. It's like a pearl necklace, stringing together moments of being fully present until all of life becomes an opportunity to hold love, share love, and experience love.

One way I bring the sacred into my life is through quiet time early on Sunday mornings. In the early hours, when the birds are just waking up and there is still dew on the rose petals, I get up and go downstairs to commune with my spirit. In those moments when the world is still, I dance, sing, chant, write, laugh, cry, feel God within me, and open to allow the energy of life to flow unobstructed through my awareness. In this way, I have reverence—a deep respect and honoring—for my soul.

LIVE THE LOVE STORY WITHIN YOU

Shangri-Love is that place within your heart where there is a pool of love that is vast and deep. It is eternal. This is your unification with Spirit and it is unchanging. By utilizing the tools in this book and contemplating the love nuggets shared here, I invite you to live with a deep devotion to your beautiful heart and to spend time truly awakening the multifaceted, infinite layers of the divine that exist within you. In doing so, you will assume full responsibility for living your love story full out.

The more you seek the love that is already within you, the more you will experience a fully integrated self, heart, mind, and life. The more you will become fully immersed in a grander picture of life, feeling whole and complete as you navigate life's ups and downs. This is the lotus flower of your heart, fully open, a radiant beacon of love and compassion. May the words here serve again and again as catalysts for love, enabling you to live in deep connection to your Shangri-Love, always.

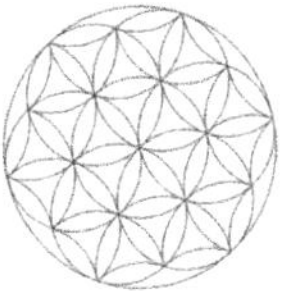

Living in Shangri-Love Activity
TEJAS MUDRA

There is a yogic mudra called the *Tejas mudra* that I use to amplify my loving heart. A mudra is a subtle hand movement, gesture, position, or pose in the yoga tradition that is used to guide energy and expand conscious awareness. The Tejas mudra, to me, resembles making a lotus flower with your hands. It's created by aligning your thumbs together facing upward and gently touching the tips of your two index fingers together, forming a subtle arch. The rest of your fingers are spread wide apart, fanning out to create a lotus-like flower. The mudra is completed by holding this gesture a few inches in front of the heart, relaxing the elbows and arms to the sides. As I hold this pose, I imagine love radiating out from my heart, shining out into the space around me and then out to my family, friends, and the world.

This pose helps me to draw attention into the center of my heart and to focus on love. It also helps me to expand the awareness of love within me, so that I have truly embodied love, received love, and awakened to the love within my own heart so that I can share it with others.

REFERENCES
(Listed in order of appearance within the chapter)

Introduction

Hilton, James. *Lost Horizon*. New York: Open Road Integrated Media. Ebook. First published by Macmillan, 1933.

Chapter One

1. Wauters, Ambika. *Chakras and Their Archetypes: Uniting Energy Awareness and Spiritual Growth*. San Francisco: Potter/TenSpeed/ Harmony, 1997. Chapter 6.

2. Jewel. "Foolish Games." *Pieces of You*, Atlantic Records, 1995. CD.

Chapter Two

1. Schucman, Helen. *A Course in Miracles*. Mill Valley, California: Foundation for Inner Peace, 1977. 191.

2. Levine, Stephen. *Unattended Sorrow: Recovering from Loss and Reviving the Heart*. Emmaus, Pennsylvania: Rodale, 2005. 19.

3. Singer, Michael A. *The Surrender Experiment: My Journey into Life's Perfection*. New York: Harmony, 2015. 10.

4. Hora, Thomas. *Beyond the Dream: Awakening to Reality*. New York: The Crossroad Publishing Company, 1996. 7.

Chapter Three

Intro quote: Tolle, Eckhart. *The Power of the Heart*. Heriot, Drew, dir. Film. 2014.

1. Dispenza, Joe. *Evolve Your Brain: The Science of Changing Your Mind*. Deerfield Beach: Health Communications, Inc., 2007. 344.

2. Villoldo, Alberto. *Illumination: The Shaman's Way of Healing.* Carlsbad: Hay House, 2010.

3. Tolle, Eckhart. *A New Earth: Awakening to Your Life's Purpose.* New York: Penguin Group, 2005. 102.

4. Cartwright, Mark. "Agni." Ancient History Encyclopedia. Ancient.eu. Web. Accessed 31 July, 2016.

5. Yeshe, Thubten. *The Bliss of Inner Fire: Heart Practice of the Six Yogas of Naropa.* Somerville, Massachusetts: Wisdom Publications, 1998, 2015. 22.

6. Chopra, Deepak, and David Simon. *The Seven Spiritual Laws of Yoga: A Practical Guide to Healing Body, Mind, and Spirit.* Hoboken: John Wiley & Sons, Inc., 2005. 149, 17, 149.

7. Roche, Lorin. *The Radiance Sutras: 112 Gateways to the Yoga of Wonder and Delight.* Boulder: Sounds True, 2014. No. 29.

Chapter Four

Intro quote: Ferrini, Paul. *The Silence of the Heart.* Greenfield, Massachusetts: Heartways Press, 1996. 60.

1. Choquette, Sonia. *The Answer Is Simple . . . Love Yourself, Live Your Spirit!* Carlsbad: Hay House, 2008. 40.

2. Castaneda, Carlos. *The Active Side of Infinity.* New York: Harper Perennial, 2000. 61.

3. Bodin, Luc, Nathalie Bodin Lamboy, and Jean Graciet. *The Book of Ho'oponopono: The Hawaiian Practice of Forgiveness and Healing.* Rochester, Vermont: Destiny Books, 2016. vii.

4. Wimberger, Lisa. *Neurosculpting: A Whole-Brain Approach to Heal Trauma, Rewrite Limiting Beliefs, and Find Wholeness.* Boulder: Sounds True, 2014.

5. Ruiz, Don Miguel and Barbara Emrys. *The Toltec Art of Life and Death: A Story of Discovery*. San Francisco: Harper Elixir, 2015.

6. Childre, Doc et al., *Heart Intelligence: Connecting with the Intuitive Guidance of the Heart*. Waterfront Press, 2016.

7. McCraty, Rollin and Doc Childre. Heartmath.com. "Coherence: Bridging Personal, Social and Global Health." *Alternative Therapies Health Med.*, 2010; 16(4):10–24. Accessed 7 June, 2016. Web.

Chapter Five

1. *"Winged Heart of the Sufi Order."* Symboldictionary.net, Accessed 29 June 2016. Web.

2. Rumi. "Stay Close, My Heart." (Rassouli, translation). Alana Fairchild. *Rumi Oracle*. Waverly, Victoria, Australia: Blue Angel Publishing, 2016.

Chapter Six

Intro quote: Rumi. Goodreads.com. Accessed 1 August 2016. Web.

1. Avila, St. Teresa. *The Interior Castle*. (M. Starr, trans.). New York, New York: Riverhead Books, 2003.

2. Bhatnagar, Sri Shyamji and Isaacs, David. *Microchakras: InnerTuning for Psychological Well-Being*. Rochester, Vermont: Inner Traditions, 2009.

3. Adyashanti, *True Meditation*. Boulder: Sounds True, 2006. CD.

4. Nhat Hahn, Thich. *True Love: A Practice for Awakening the Heart*. Boston: Shambhala Publications, Inc., 1997.

Chapter Seven

1. Brach, Tara. *Radical Acceptance: Embracing Your Life with the Heart of a Buddha*. New York: Bantam Books, 2003.

2. Holmes, Ernest. *Science of Mind*. United Kingdom: Stellar Books, 2014 edition.

3. Dogen, Zenmaster. Quoted in Nikolaj Flor Rotne and Didde Flor Rotne. *Inner Peace and Contagious Happiness for Education's Superstars.* Berkeley: Parallax Press, 2013.

4. Gilbert, Elizabeth. *Big Magic: Creative Living beyond Fear.* New York: Riverhead Books, 2015.

5. Shinoda Bolen, Jean. *Goddesses in Everywoman: Powerful Archetypes in Women's Lives.* New York: Harper Perennial, 2004. 25.

6. Virtue, Doreen. *Archangels and Ascended Masters: A Guide to Working and Healing with Divinities and Deities.* Carlsbad: Hay House, 2004. 141–142, 143

Chapter Eight

Intro quote: Nepo, Mark. *Seven Thousand Ways to Listen: Staying Close to What Is Sacred.* New York: Atria, 2012. 256.

1. Kelder, Peter. *Ancient Secret of the Fountain of Youth, Book 2.* New York: Doubleday, 1999.

2. Goldthwait, John. *Purifying the Heart.* Anantapur District, India: Sri Sathya Sai Sadhana Trust, 2010.

3. Levine, Stephen and Ondrea Levine. *Embracing the Beloved: Relationship as a Path of Awakening.* New York: Doubleday, 1995. 45.

4. Williamson, Marianne. *Enchanted Love: The Mystical Power of Intimate Relationships.* New York: Simon & Schuster, 1999. 132.

5. Krishna Das. *Sri Argala Stotram/Show Me Love.* Krishna Das Music, 2014. CD.

Chapter Nine

Intro quote: Hafiz. Goodreads.com. Accessed 1 August, 2016. Web.

1. Bodhi, Bhikkhu. "The Middle Way." Beyondthenet.net. 31 July, 2016. Web.

2. Proust, Marcel. Azquotes.com. Web. 31 July, 2016.

3. Brown, Michael. *The Presence Process: A Healing Journey into Present Moment Awareness*, Revised Edition. Vancouver: Namaste Publishing, 2010.

4. Tzu, Lao (Laozi). Azquotes.com. Web. 31 July, 2016.

About the Artist

Maddie Jazwierska has been creating art since before she could walk. While still in diapers, she would spend countless hours drawing minuscule circles on paper. She's been known to turn her bedroom wall into a celestial portal and to don a mermaid tail for trial at the athletic club. A majority of the illustrations created for this book were completed at age thirteen. For more of her artwork, please visit www.madelynart.com.

Made in the USA
Monee, IL
07 July 2026

56549103R00115